•100 Calorie•
Contents

·Sweet· Treats

Banana and Ginger Cream Mousse

1 teaspoon unflavored gelatin
1/4 cup fat-free half-and-half
2 tablespoons (1/2 ounce) finely chopped crystallized ginger
1 cup thawed reduced-fat whipped topping
1 large banana, thinly sliced
1 whole low-fat graham cracker, crushed

1. Sprinkle gelatin over half-and-half in medium bowl. Let stand 5 minutes or until gelatin softens. Stir in ginger; fold in whipped topping. Chill 1 hour or until firm but not stiff.

2. Gently stir ginger cream. Divide among four dessert bowls. Top each with one fourth of banana slices and one fourth of cracker crumbs. Serve immediately.

Makes 4 servings

Nutrients per Serving: Calories: 90, Calories from Fat: 30%, Total Fat: 3g, Saturated Fat: 3g, Cholesterol: 0mg, Sodium: 40mg, Carbohydrate: 16g, Fiber: 1g, Protein: 2g

• Sweet **Treats** •

Watermelon Granita

5 cups cubed seeded watermelon
¹⁄₂ cup sugar
1 envelope (¹⁄₄ ounce) unflavored gelatin
¹⁄₂ cup cranberry juice cocktail

1. Process watermelon in food processor until nearly smooth. (You should have about 3¹⁄₃ cups.)

2. Combine sugar and gelatin in small saucepan. Gradually stir in juice. Cook and stir over low heat until gelatin dissolves. Add to watermelon purée in food processor; process until combined. Pour into 8-inch square baking dish. Cover and freeze about 5 hours or until firm.

3. Break watermelon mixture into chunks in baking dish. Freeze about 3 hours or until firm. To serve, stir and scrape granita with fork to create icy texture. Spoon into dessert dishes. *Makes 8 servings*

Nutrients per Serving (¹⁄₂ cup): Calories: 88, Calories from Fat: 0%, Total Fat: 0g, Saturated Fat: 0g, Cholesterol: 0mg, Sodium: 5mg, Carbohydrate: 22g, Fiber: <1g, Protein: 1g

Citrus Fruit Toss

¹⁄₄ cup dried cranberries
¹⁄₄ cup water
2 cups red grapefruit sections, drained
2 tablespoons sucralose-based sugar substitute
2 tablespoons fresh mint leaves, chopped
1 tablespoon lime juice

1. Combine cranberries and water in medium microwavable bowl. Microwave on HIGH 1 minute; let stand 5 minutes. Drain well.

2. Combine cranberries, grapefruit, sugar substitute, mint and lime juice in same bowl; toss gently. Let stand 5 minutes before serving. *Makes 4 servings*

Nutrients per Serving (¹⁄₂ cup): Calories: 74, Calories from Fat: 2%, Total Fat: <1g, Saturated Fat: <1g, Cholesterol: 0mg, Sodium: <1mg, Carbohydrate: 20g, Fiber: 2g, Protein: <1g

Watermelon Granita

• Sweet **Treats** •

Peach Turnovers

2 cups chopped peeled fresh peaches or frozen unsweetened peach slices, thawed, drained and chopped

2 tablespoons granulated sugar

1 tablespoon all-purpose flour

¼ teaspoon vanilla

⅛ teaspoon ground nutmeg

6 sheets (about 12×8¼-inches each) frozen phyllo dough, thawed
Nonstick cooking spray

1 tablespoon powdered sugar

1. Preheat oven to 375°F. Line baking sheet with parchment paper or foil. Combine peaches, granulated sugar, flour, vanilla and nutmeg in medium bowl; toss until combined.

2. Place one sheet phyllo dough on damp kitchen towel. (Keep remaining dough covered.) Lightly spray dough with cooking spray. Top with second sheet phyllo. Using sharp knife or pizza cutter, cut into two lengthwise strips, each about 12×4 inches.

3. For each turnover, spoon about ⅓ cup peach mixture onto dough about 1 inch from end of each strip. Fold one corner over filling to make triangle. Continue folding as you would fold a flag to form triangle that encloses filling. Repeat with remaining dough and filling. Place on prepared baking sheet. Spray tops of turnovers with cooking spray.

4. Bake about 17 minutes or until golden brown. Cool on wire rack 10 minutes. Sprinkle with powdered sugar. Serve warm.   *Makes 6 servings*

Nutrients per Serving: Calories: 103, Calories from Fat: 8%, Total Fat: 1g, Saturated Fat: <1g, Cholesterol: 0mg, Sodium: 92mg, Carbohydrate: 21g, Fiber: 1g, Protein: 2g

Peach Turnovers

33 calories

• Sweet **Treats** •

Chocolate Cream Dessert Dip

2 cups fat-free (skim) milk
1 package (4-serving size) chocolate fat-free sugar-free instant pudding
    and pie filling mix
1 container (8 ounces) thawed fat-free whipped topping
2 tablespoons chocolate chips, finely chopped
    Chocolate curls (optional)

Beat milk and pudding mix in medium bowl with electric mixer at medium speed
2 minutes. Stir in whipped topping and chocolate chips until well blended.
Refrigerate until ready to serve. Garnish with chocolate curls.   *Makes 24 servings*

Nutrients per Serving (2 tablespoons dip without fruit): Calories: 33,
Calories from Fat: 9%, Total Fat: <1g, Saturated Fat: <1g, Cholesterol: <1mg,
Sodium: 38mg, Carbohydrate: 6g, Fiber: 0g, Protein: <1g

Choco-Cherry Chill

62 calories

1 can (about 14 ounces) pitted tart cherries in water, undrained
1¹/₂ cups frozen pitted unsweetened dark Bing cherries
1 cup fat-free half-and-half
¹/₂ cup reduced-sugar chocolate syrup
1 teaspoon vanilla
    Fresh mint leaves (optional)
    Additional frozen cherries (optional)

1. Place tart cherries with liquid, Bing cherries, half-and-half, chocolate syrup and
vanilla in blender; blend until smooth.

2. Freeze cherry mixture in ice cream maker according to manufacturer's directions.

3. Let stand 15 minutes at room temperature before serving. Garnish each serving
with mint and additional cherry.   *Makes 8 servings*

Nutrients per Serving (¹/₂ cup): Calories: 62, Calories from Fat: 2%, Total Fat: <1g,
Saturated Fat: <1g, Cholesterol: 4mg, Sodium: 41mg, Carbohydrate: 14g, Fiber: 1g,
Protein: 2g

Chocolate Cream Dessert Dip

Cheesecake Bites with Ginger-Berry Topping

8 gingersnap cookies (2-inch diameter)
4 ounces fat-free cream cheese, softened
1 package (4-serving size) cheesecake-flavored fat-free sugar-free instant pudding and pie filling mix
1¼ cups fat-free (skim) milk

Ginger-Berry Topping
½ cup sugar-free blueberry preserves
¾ cup fresh or thawed frozen blueberries
1 teaspoon ground ginger

1. Line 24 mini (1¾-inch) muffin cups with paper baking cups. Break gingersnaps into pieces; process in food processor to make about ½ cup fine crumbs. Place 1 teaspoon crumbs in each cup.

2. Beat cream cheese in medium bowl with electric mixer at low speed until smooth. Add pudding mix and milk; beat at high speed 2 minutes or until smooth and creamy. Spoon rounded tablespoonful cream cheese mixture into each cup. Place pan in freezer while preparing topping.

3. For Ginger-Berry Topping, place preserves in medium microwavable bowl. Microwave on HIGH 15 seconds. Stir in blueberries and ginger.

4. Spoon 1 teaspoon topping over each cheesecake bite. Serve immediately or cover and refrigerate up to 2 hours. *Makes 8 servings*

Nutrients per Serving (3 pieces): Calories: 87, Calories from Fat: 10%, Total Fat: 1g, Saturated Fat: 0g, Cholesterol: 2mg, Sodium: 305mg, Carbohydrate: 18g, Fiber: 1g, Protein: 4g

Cheesecake Bites with Ginger-Berry Topping

• Sweet **Treats** •

Grapefruit Sorbet

1 large pink grapefruit
$\frac{1}{2}$ cup apple juice
$1\frac{1}{2}$ tablespoons sugar

1. Peel grapefruit and remove white pith. Cut into segments over bowl to catch juices, removing membranes between segments. Combine grapefruit, grapefruit juice, apple juice and sugar in food processor or blender; process until smooth.

2. Freeze grapefruit mixture in ice cream maker according to manufacturer's directions. Serve immediately. *Makes 4 servings*

Nutrients per Serving ($\frac{1}{3}$ cup): Calories: 59, Calories from Fat: 0%, Total Fat: 0g, Saturated Fat: 0g, Cholesterol: 0mg, Sodium: 0mg, Carbohydrate: 15g, Fiber: 1g, Protein: <1g

Baked Pear Dessert

$\frac{1}{3}$ cup unsweetened apple cider or apple juice, divided
2 tablespoons dried cranberries or raisins
1 tablespoon toasted sliced almonds
$\frac{1}{8}$ teaspoon ground cinnamon
1 medium unpeeled pear (about 6 ounces), cut in half lengthwise and cored
$\frac{1}{2}$ cup vanilla low-fat sugar-free ice cream or frozen yogurt

1. Preheat oven to 350°F. Combine 1 tablespoon cider, cranberries, almonds and cinnamon in small bowl.

2. Place pear halves, cut sides up, in small baking dish. Evenly mound almond mixture on top of pear halves. Pour remaining cider into dish around pear halves; cover with foil.

3. Bake 35 to 40 minutes or until pears are soft, spooning cider in dish over pears once or twice during baking. Serve warm with ice cream. *Makes 2 servings*

Nutrients per Serving (1 pear half with $\frac{1}{4}$ cup ice cream): Calories: 87, Calories from Fat: 19%, Total Fat: 2g, Saturated Fat: <1g, Cholesterol: 3mg, Sodium: 13mg, Carbohydrate: 16g, Fiber: 1g, Protein: 1g

Strawberry and Peach Crisp

1 cup frozen unsweetened peach slices, thawed and cut into 1-inch pieces
1 cup sliced fresh strawberries
3 teaspoons sugar, divided
¼ cup bran cereal flakes
2 tablespoons old-fashioned oats
1 tablespoon all-purpose flour
⅛ teaspoon ground cinnamon
⅛ teaspoon salt
2 teaspoons unsalted margarine, cut into small pieces

1. Preheat oven to 325°F. Spray 1- to 1½-quart baking dish with nonstick cooking spray.

2. Combine peaches and strawberries in medium bowl. Sprinkle with 1 teaspoon sugar. Transfer fruit to prepared baking dish.

3. Combine cereal, oats, flour, cinnamon and salt in small bowl. Stir in remaining 2 teaspoons sugar. Add margarine; stir with fork until mixture resembles coarse crumbs. Sprinkle over fruit in baking dish.

4. Bake 20 minutes or until fruit is hot and topping is slightly browned.

Makes 4 servings

Variation: Substitute 2 teaspoons packed brown sugar for the 2 teaspoons granulated sugar in the topping.

Variation: For a strawberry crisp, omit the peaches and use 2 cups strawberries in the recipe.

Nutrients per Serving (½ cup): Calories: 80, Calories from Fat: 24%, Total Fat: 2g, Saturated Fat: <1g, Cholesterol: 0mg, Sodium: 83mg, Carbohydrate: 15g, Fiber: 3g, Protein: 1g

Strawberry and Peach Crisp

• Sweet **Treats** •

Chocolate Chip Frozen Yogurt

1 cup plain fat-free yogurt
$^1/_2$ cup fat-free half-and-half
2 tablespoons sugar
$^1/_4$ teaspoon vanilla
$^1/_4$ cup mini chocolate chips

1. Combine yogurt, half-and-half, sugar and vanilla in medium bowl; mix well.

2. Freeze yogurt mixture in ice cream maker according to manufacturer's directions until soft. Add chocolate chips; freeze until firm. *Makes 6 servings*

Nutrients per Serving ($^1/_3$ cup): Calories: 87, Calories from Fat: 21%, Total Fat: 2g, Saturated Fat: 1g, Cholesterol: 4mg, Sodium: 52mg, Carbohydrate: 14g, Fiber: <1g, Protein: 3g

Berries with Creamy Lemon Ricotta

12 ounces (about 1$^1/_2$ cups) reduced-fat ricotta cheese
3 tablespoons sugar
1 teaspoon grated lemon peel, plus additional for garnish
2 tablespoons lemon juice
1 teaspoon vanilla
2 cups fresh blueberries and raspberries
Fresh mint leaves (optional)

1. Stir ricotta, sugar, 1 teaspoon lemon peel, lemon juice and vanilla in medium bowl until well blended. Cover and refrigerate up to 2 hours.

2. Spoon ricotta mixture into six dessert dishes. Top with berries. Garnish with additional lemon peel and mint. *Makes 6 servings*

Nutrients per Serving ($^1/_3$ cup ricotta mixture with $^1/_3$ cup berries): Calories: 110, Calories from Fat: 25%, Total Fat: 3g, Saturated Fat: 2g, Cholesterol: 18mg, Sodium: 138mg, Carbohydrate: 17g, Fiber: 1g, Protein: 7g

Chocolate Chip Frozen Yogurt

Summer Strawberry Orange Cups

2 cups fresh strawberries, divided
1 envelope ($^1/_4$ ounce) unflavored gelatin
2 tablespoons cold water
2 tablespoons boiling water
1$^1/_2$ cups reduced-fat (2%) milk
$^1/_2$ cup frozen orange juice concentrate
1 teaspoon vanilla
Fresh mint leaves (optional)

1. Cut 1 cup strawberries into thin slices; place in bottom of six 8-ounce dessert dishes or custard cups.

2. Combine gelatin and cold water in small bowl; let stand 5 minutes. Add boiling water; stir until gelatin is completely dissolved.

3. Combine milk, orange juice concentrate and vanilla in medium bowl; mix well. Let stand at room temperature 20 minutes. Stir in gelatin mixture until well blended. Pour evenly over sliced strawberries in dishes. Refrigerate 2 hours or until completely set.

4. Slice remaining 1 cup strawberries; arrange on top of each dessert. Garnish with mint. *Makes 6 servings*

Nutrients per Serving: Calories: 89, Calories from Fat: 10%, Total Fat: 1g, Saturated Fat: <1g, Cholesterol: 5mg, Sodium: 29mg, Carbohydrate: 16g, Fiber: 1g, Protein: 4g

Summer Strawberry Orange Cups

• Sweet **Treats** •

Mango Mousse

1 envelope (¼ ounce) unflavored gelatin
½ cup cold water
½ cup boiling water
2½ cups mango chunks (see Note), plus additional for garnish
2 tablespoons sugar
2 teaspoons lemon juice
¾ cup thawed fat-free whipped topping, divided

1. Combine gelatin and cold water in small bowl; let stand 5 minutes. Add boiling water; stir until gelatin is completely dissolved. Set aside to cool.

2. Combine 2½ cups mango, sugar and lemon juice in blender or food processor; blend until smooth. Spoon mango mixture into large bowl; stir in gelatin mixture. Gently fold in ½ cup whipped topping. Refrigerate 1 hour or until firm.

3. Spoon into eight dessert cups. Top each serving with 1½ teaspoons whipped topping. Garnish with additional mango chunks. *Makes 8 servings*

Note: Use 2 medium to medium-large fresh mangos or a 1-pound package of frozen mango chunks packed without sugar. Measure out 2½ cups.

Nutrients per Serving (⅓ cup): Calories: 70, Calories from Fat: 0%, Total Fat: 0g, Saturated Fat: 0g, Cholesterol: 0mg, Sodium: 3mg, Carbohydrate: 17g, Fiber: 1g, Protein: 1g

 **Tip**

Cutting a mango requires cutting around the large flat seed that runs the length of the fruit. Place the mango, stem side down, on a cutting board with the narrow end facing you. Cut through the rounded sides about ¼ inch from the top center. With the peel still on, cut parallel slices into the fruit of the rounded sides, then scoop out the slices with a spoon.

Mango Mousse

Peaches with Raspberry Sauce

1 cup fresh raspberries
1/2 cup water
1/4 cup sugar substitute
6 fresh peach halves
1/3 cup vanilla fat-free yogurt

1. Combine raspberries, water and sugar substitute in small saucepan. Bring to a boil over medium-high heat, stirring frequently. Boil 1 minute. Transfer to food processor or blender; process until smooth. Set aside 15 minutes to cool.

2. Drizzle 1/4 cup raspberry sauce onto each of six serving dishes. Place one peach half on each dish. Spoon about 2 1/2 teaspoons yogurt over each peach half.

Makes 6 servings

Nutrients per Serving (1 peach half with 1/4 cup raspberry sauce and about 2 1/2 teaspoons yogurt): Calories: 41, Calories from Fat: 0%, Total Fat: 0g, Saturated Fat: 0g, Cholesterol: <1mg, Sodium: 9mg, Carbohydrate: 10g, Fiber: 2g, Protein: 1g

Strawberries with Honeyed Yogurt Sauce

1 cup plain low-fat yogurt
1 tablespoon orange juice
1 to 2 teaspoons honey
Ground cinnamon
1 quart fresh strawberries, stems removed

Combine yogurt, juice, honey and cinnamon to taste in small bowl; mix well. Serve sauce over strawberries.

Makes 4 servings

Nutrients per Serving (1 cup strawberries with about 1/4 cup sauce): Calories: 88, Calories from Fat: 10%, Total Fat: 1g, Saturated Fat: 1g, Cholesterol: 4mg, Sodium: 41mg, Carbohydrate: 16g, Fiber: 4g, Protein: 4g

Peaches with Raspberry Sauce

• Sweet **Treats** •

Mocha Cream Tartlets

- **1 package (4-serving size) chocolate fat-free sugar-free cook-and-serve pudding and pie filling mix**
- **2 cups fat-free half-and-half, divided**
- **1½ teaspoons instant coffee granules**
- **⅛ teaspoon ground cinnamon**
- **½ cup old-fashioned oats**
- **½ cup all-purpose flour**
- **¼ cup graham cracker crumbs**
- **1 tablespoon sugar**
- **¼ cup unsalted margarine, melted**
- **1½ cups thawed reduced-fat whipped topping**
- **16 chocolate-covered espresso beans (optional)**

1. Combine pudding mix and ½ cup half-and-half in medium saucepan; stir until smooth. Stir in remaining 1½ cups half-and-half, coffee and cinnamon. Bring to a boil over medium-high heat, stirring constantly. Remove from heat; spoon into medium bowl and refrigerate at least 1 hour.

2. Preheat oven to 375°F. Line 16 standard (2½-inch) muffin cups with paper baking cups.

3. Combine oats, flour, cracker crumbs and sugar in medium bowl. Stir in margarine until mixture comes together when pressed. Spoon 1 tablespoon crumb mixture into each cup; press to form crust. Bake 13 minutes or until crusts are golden brown and firm. Cool completely in pan on wire rack.

4. To assemble tartlets, gently fold whipped topping into chocolate pudding. Spoon mixture into cooled crusts. Garnish with espresso beans.   *Makes 16 servings*

Note: The filling in the tartlets may be soft or firm depending on the pudding mix. For a firmer filling, chill the assembled tartlets for 2 or more hours.

Nutrients per Serving (1 tartlet): Calories: 100, Calories from Fat: 45%, Total Fat: 5g, Saturated Fat: 2g, Cholesterol: 0mg, Sodium: 70mg, Carbohydrate: 13g, Fiber: 0g, Protein: 2g

• Sweet **Treats** •

Citrus Tapioca Pudding

   2 navel oranges
2$^1/_2$ cups fat-free (skim) milk
   $^1/_3$ cup sugar
   $^1/_4$ cup cholesterol-free egg substitute
   3 tablespoons quick-cooking tapioca
   $^1/_2$ teaspoon almond extract
     Ground cinnamon or nutmeg
     Orange slices (optional)

1. Grate peel of 1 orange into medium saucepan. Add milk, sugar, egg substitute and tapioca; let stand 5 minutes. Cook and stir over medium heat 5 minutes or until mixture comes to a boil. Remove from heat; stir in almond extract. Let stand 20 minutes. Stir well; cool to room temperature. Cover and refrigerate at least 2 hours.

2. Peel and dice oranges. Stir tapioca mixture; fold in oranges. Spoon into eight dessert dishes. Sprinkle each serving with cinnamon; garnish with orange slices.

Makes 8 servings

Nutrients per Serving: Calories: 89, Calories from Fat: 2%, Total Fat: <1g, Saturated Fat: <1g, Cholesterol: 1mg, Sodium: 50mg, Carbohydrate: 19g, Fiber: 1g, Protein: 4g

Cantaloupe Sorbet

   6 cups cubed fresh cantaloupe
   $^1/_3$ cup light corn syrup
   3 tablespoons lime juice

1. Process cantaloupe in food processor until puréed. (You should have about 3 cups.) Add corn syrup and lime juice; process until combined.

2. Freeze cantaloupe mixture in ice cream maker according to manufacturer's directions.

Makes 8 servings

Nutrients per Serving ($^1/_2$ cup): Calories: 103, Calories from Fat: 0%, Total Fat: 0g, Saturated Fat: 0g, Cholesterol: 0mg, Sodium: 29mg, Carbohydrate: 26g, Fiber: 1g, Protein: 2g

Citrus Tapioca Pudding

·Cookies,·
Bars & Bites

Angelic Macaroons

1 package (16 ounces) angel food cake mix
$1/2$ cup cold water
1 teaspoon almond extract
1 package (14 ounces) sweetened flaked coconut
$1/2$ cup slivered almonds, coarsley chopped

1. Preheat oven to 325°F. Line cookie sheets with parchment paper.

2. Beat cake mix, water and almond extract in large bowl with electric mixer at medium speed until well blended. Add half of coconut; beat until blended. Add remaining coconut and almonds; beat until well blended. Drop dough by tablespoonfuls about 2 inches apart onto prepared cookie sheets.

3. Bake 22 to 25 minutes or until golden brown. Cool cookies on cookie sheets 3 minutes. Remove to wire racks; cool completely. *Makes 40 cookies*

Nutrients per Serving (1 cookie): Calories: 94, Calories from Fat: 38%, Total Fat: 4g, Saturated Fat: 3g, Cholesterol: 0mg, Sodium: 86mg, Carbohydrate: 14g, Fiber: 1g, Protein: 2g

• Cookies, **Bars & Bites** •

S'more Treats

2^1/$_2$ cups cocoa-flavored sweetened rice cereal
6 whole low-fat honey graham crackers
3 tablespoons margarine
1 tablespoon sucralose-brown sugar blend
3^1/$_2$ cups mini marshmallows, divided
1 square (1 ounce) semisweet or milk chocolate, melted (optional)

1. Lightly spray 9-inch square baking pan with nonstick cooking spray. Place cereal in large bowl. Crumble graham crackers into ^{1}/$_4$-inch pieces; add to bowl. Toss to combine.

2. Combine margarine and sucralose-brown sugar blend in large microwavable bowl; microwave on HIGH 25 to 30 seconds or until margarine is melted. Add 2^1/$_2$ cups marshmallows; microwave on HIGH 1^1/$_2$ to 2 minutes or until marshmallows are melted, stirring after 1 minute. Stir until mixture is smooth.

3. Add marshmallow mixture to cereal mixture; stir to coat. Add remaining 1 cup marshmallows; stir until blended. Press evenly into prepared pan using waxed paper. Cool completely. Drizzle with chocolate, if desired. Cut into squares.

Makes 16 squares

Nutrients per Serving (1 square): Calories: 89, Calories from Fat: 20%, Total Fat: 2g, Saturated Fat: <1g, Cholesterol: 0mg, Sodium: 79mg, Carbohydrate: 16g, Fiber: 0g, Protein: <1g

 For a slightly thicker treat, use an 8-inch square baking pan. Or for some variety, cut out fun shapes using a greased 2-inch cookie cutter.

S'more Treats

• Cookies, **Bars & Bites** •

Cinnamon Flats

1³/₄ cups all-purpose flour
¹/₂ cup sugar
1¹/₂ teaspoons ground cinnamon
¹/₄ teaspoon salt
¹/₄ teaspoon ground nutmeg
¹/₂ cup (1 stick) cold margarine
3 egg whites, divided
1 teaspoon vanilla
1 teaspoon water
Sugar Glaze (recipe follows)

1. Preheat oven to 350°F. Spray 15×10-inch jelly-roll pan with nonstick cooking spray. Combine flour, sugar, cinnamon, salt and nutmeg in medium bowl. Cut in margarine with pastry blender or two knives until mixture forms coarse crumbs. Beat in 2 egg whites and vanilla; mix to form soft dough.

2. Divide dough into six equal pieces; place on prepared pan. Press dough evenly to edges of pan; smooth top of dough with spatula. Mix remaining egg white and water in small cup; brush over dough. Lightly score dough into 2×1¹/₂-inch pieces.

3. Bake 20 to 25 minutes or until lightly browned and firm. While still warm, cut along score lines into pieces; drizzle with Sugar Glaze. Let stand 15 minutes or until glaze is firm before removing from pan. *Makes 50 cookies*

Sugar Glaze

1¹/₂ cups powdered sugar
2 to 3 tablespoons fat-free (skim) milk
1 teaspoon vanilla

Combine sugar, 2 tablespoons milk and vanilla in small bowl. If glaze is too thick, add remaining 1 tablespoon milk. *Makes about ³/₄ cup*

Nutrients per Serving (1 cookie): Calories: 48, Calories from Fat: 18%, Total Fat: 1g, Saturated Fat: <1g, Cholesterol: <1mg, Sodium: 35mg, Carbohydrate: 9g, Fiber: <1g, Protein: 1g

Cinnamon Flats

• Cookies, **Bars & Bites** •

Cocoa-Almond Meringue Puffs

2 tablespoons granulated sugar
3 packets sugar substitute
1¹/₂ teaspoons unsweetened cocoa powder
2 egg whites, at room temperature
¹/₂ teaspoon vanilla
¹/₄ teaspoon cream of tartar
¹/₄ teaspoon almond extract
¹/₈ teaspoon salt
1¹/₂ ounces (7 tablespoons) sliced almonds
3 tablespoons seedless raspberry fruit spread

1. Preheat oven to 275°F. Line cookie sheet with foil. Combine granulated sugar, sugar substitute and cocoa in small bowl.

2. Beat egg whites in medium bowl with electric mixer at high speed until foamy. Add vanilla, cream of tartar, almond extract and salt; beat until soft peaks form. Add sugar mixture, 1 tablespoon at a time, beating until stiff peaks form.

3. Spoon 15 equal mounds egg white mixture onto prepared cookie sheet. Sprinkle with almonds.

4. Bake 1 hour. Turn oven off but do not open door. Leave cookies in oven 2 hours or until completely dry. Remove from oven; cool completely.

5. Spoon about ¹/₂ teaspoon fruit spread onto each cookie just before serving.

Makes 15 cookies

Tip: These cookies are best if eaten the same day they're made. If necessary, store them in an airtight container, adding the fruit spread just before serving.

Nutrients per Serving (1 cookie): Calories: 34, Calories from Fat: 26%, Total Fat: 1g, Saturated Fat: <1g, Cholesterol: 0mg, Sodium: 27mg, Carbohydrate: 5g, Fiber: <1g, Protein: 1g

•Cookies, **Bars & Bites**•

Lemon Almond Biscotti

$1/3$ cup margarine, softened
$2/3$ cup sugar
  2 tablespoons grated lemon peel
  1 teaspoon baking powder
$1/2$ teaspoon baking soda
$1/8$ teaspoon salt
  2 eggs
$2^{1}/2$ cups all-purpose flour
$1/2$ cup slivered almonds

1. Preheat oven to 375°F. Beat margarine in large bowl with electric mixer at medium speed 30 seconds. Add sugar, lemon peel, baking powder, baking soda and salt; beat until well blended. Beat in eggs. Add flour; beat until crumbly. (Dough will be fairly dry.) Stir in almonds.

2. Shape dough into two 9-inch logs. Flatten logs to $1^{1}/2$-inch thickness. Place on nonstick cookie sheet.

3. Bake 20 minutes or until toothpick inserted into centers of logs comes out clean. Cool on cookie sheet 1 hour.

4. Cut each log crosswise into 16 ($1/2$-inch) slices. Place slices, cut side down, on cookie sheet; bake 8 minutes. Turn and bake 8 minutes or until crisp and golden. Cool completely on wire racks. Store in airtight container up to 3 days.

Makes 32 biscotti

Nutrients per Serving (1 biscotti): Calories: 85, Calories from Fat: 35%, Total Fat: 3g, Saturated Fat: <1g, Cholesterol: 13mg, Sodium: 70mg, Carbohydrate: 12g, Fiber: <1g, Protein: 2g

Lemon Almond Biscotti

Raspberry Oat Bars

1 cup old-fashioned oats
$^1/_2$ cup all-purpose flour
$^1/_2$ cup soy-protein cereal clusters
2 tablespoons sugar
$^1/_4$ teaspoon ground cinnamon
$^1/_8$ teaspoon salt
5 tablespoons margarine, cut into small pieces
$^3/_4$ cup raspberry fruit spread

1. Preheat oven to 350°F. Spray 8-inch square baking pan with nonstick cooking spray.

2. Combine oats, flour, cereal, sugar, cinnamon and salt in food processor; process until blended. Add margarine; process with on/off pulses just until coarse crumbs form. Set aside $^1/_2$ cup crumbs for topping. Press remaining crumbs onto bottom of prepared pan.

3. Bake 15 minutes. Spread fruit spread over crust; sprinkle with reserved crumbs. Bake 20 to 25 minutes or until edges are browned and fruit spread is firm. Cool slightly in pan on wire rack. Cut into bars. *Makes 20 bars*

Nutrients per Serving (1 bar): Calories: 80, Calories from Fat: 34%, Total Fat: 3g, Saturated Fat: <1g, Cholesterol: 0mg, Sodium: 50mg, Carbohydrate: 13g, Fiber: 1g, Protein: 1g

Raspberry Oat Bars

•Cookies, **Bars & Bites**•

Apple & Raisin Softies

1^3/$_4$ cups all-purpose flour
^{1}/$_2$ cup whole wheat flour
1^1/$_2$ teaspoons pumpkin pie spice
^{1}/$_2$ teaspoon baking soda
^{1}/$_2$ teaspoon baking powder
^{3}/$_4$ cup (1^1/$_2$ sticks) margarine, softened
^{3}/$_4$ cup packed sucralose-brown sugar blend
1 egg
^{1}/$_2$ cup unsweetened applesauce
1 small apple, peeled, cored and finely chopped
1 cup walnuts, chopped
^{3}/$_4$ cup raisins

1. Preheat oven to 375°F. Line cookie sheets with parchment paper. Combine all-purpose flour, whole wheat flour, pumpkin pie spice, baking soda and baking powder in medium bowl.

2. Beat margarine and sucralose-brown sugar blend in large bowl with electric mixer at medium speed until blended. Add egg; beat until blended. Stir in applesauce. Gradually add flour mixture; beat until well blended. Stir in apple, walnuts and raisins.

3. Drop dough by tablespoonfuls about 2 inches apart onto prepared cookie sheets. Gently flatten with back of spoon.

4. Bake 14 to 16 minutes or until deep golden brown. Cool cookies on cookie sheets 5 minutes. Remove to wire racks; cool completely.   *Makes 36 cookies*

Nutrients per Serving (1 cookie): Calories: 107, Calories from Fat: 50%, Total Fat: 6g, Saturated Fat: 1g, Cholesterol: 6mg, Sodium: 71mg, Carbohydrate: 12g, Fiber: 1g, Protein: 2g

Apple & Raisin Softies

• Cookies, **Bars & Bites** •

Pistachio Pinwheels

1 package (8 ounces) reduced-fat cream cheese, softened
$1/2$ cup (1 stick) soft baking butter with canola oil
2 cups all-purpose flour
3 tablespoons apricot fruit spread
1 tablespoon water
2 tablespoons sugar
$1/4$ teaspoon ground cinnamon
$1/2$ cup finely chopped pistachios, toasted*
Nonstick cooking spray

To toast nuts, spread in single layer on baking sheet. Bake in preheated 350°F oven 5 to 7 minutes or until golden brown, stirring frequently.

1. Preheat oven to 350°F. Line cookie sheets with parchment paper.

2. Beat cream cheese in large bowl with electric mixer at low speed 30 seconds or until smooth. Beat in butter until well blended. Add flour in three batches, beating at low speed until blended. Divide dough into two equal portions; shape into rectangles. Wrap in plastic wrap; refrigerate 20 minutes.

3. Stir fruit spread and water in small bowl. Combine sugar and cinnamon in another small bowl.

4. Roll out each piece of dough into 12×10-inch rectangle on lightly floured surface. Spread 2 tablespoons apricot mixture onto each rectangle. Sprinkle each with $1^1/2$ teaspoons sugar-cinnamon mixture and $1/4$ cup pistachios. Cut each dough rectangle in half lengthwise into two 12×5-inch pieces. Roll up each piece jelly-roll style, starting with long side.

5. Cut each roll into 16 slices. Place slices on prepared cookie sheets. Spray tops of cookies with cooking spray; sprinkle with remaining sugar-cinnamon mixture.

6. Bake 16 minutes or until golden. Cool cookies on cookie sheets 2 minutes. Remove to wire racks; cool completely. *Makes 64 cookies*

Nutrients per Serving (1 cookie): Calories: 45, Calories from Fat: 60%, Total Fat: 3g, Saturated Fat: <1g, Cholesterol: 3mg, Sodium: 34mg, Carbohydrate: 5g, Fiber: <1g, Protein: 1g

• Cookies, **Bars & Bites** •

PM Snack Bars

3 tablespoons creamy peanut butter
2 tablespoons molasses
2 egg whites
2 tablespoons ground flax seeds
4 cups crisp rice cereal
$^1/_2$ cup sliced almonds
1 ounce bittersweet chocolate, melted

1. Preheat oven to 350°F. Spray 9-inch square baking pan with nonstick cooking spray. Place peanut butter in small microwavable bowl; microwave on LOW (30%) 30 seconds or until peanut butter is melted. Stir in molasses; cool.

2. Place egg whites and flax seeds in blender; blend until foamy. Pour into large bowl. Add peanut butter mixture; stir until smooth. Stir in cereal and almonds until cereal is evenly coated. Press cereal mixture into prepared pan.

3. Bake 20 to 25 minutes or until lightly browned. Cool completely in pan on wire rack. Cut into bars. Drizzle melted chocolate over bars. *Makes 16 bars*

Tip: Look for ground flax seeds in large supermarkets or health food stores. You may also buy whole flax seeds and grind them in a coffee mill or blender.

Nutrients per Serving (1 bar): Calories: 91, Calories from Fat: 41%, Total Fat: 4g, Saturated Fat: 1g, Cholesterol: <1mg, Sodium: 24mg, Carbohydrate: 11g, Fiber: 1g, Protein: 3g

Tropical Sugar Cookie Bars

1 package (17½ ounces) sugar cookie mix
⅓ cup canola oil
1 egg
½ cup apricot fruit spread
1 teaspoon grated fresh ginger
1 can (8 ounces) pineapple tidbits, drained
1 mango, peeled, seeded and diced
1 medium kiwi, peeled and diced
2 cups fresh strawberries, stemmed and diced

1. Preheat oven to 350°F. Line bottom and sides of 13×9-inch baking pan with foil. Spray foil with nonstick cooking spray.

2. Stir cookie mix, oil and egg in medium bowl until well mixed. Spread dough evenly in prepared pan.

3. Bake 23 minutes or until golden. Gently lift cookie out of pan using foil. Cool completely on wire rack.

4. Place fruit spread in small microwavable bowl. Microwave on HIGH 1 minute or until slightly melted. Stir in ginger. Spread apricot mixture evenly over cookie. Arrange fruit over top. Cut into bars. *Makes 24 bars*

Nutrients per Serving (1 bar with ⅓ cup fruit): Calories: 68, Calories from Fat: 53%, Total Fat: 4g, Saturated Fat: <1g, Cholesterol: 9mg, Sodium: 12mg, Carbohydrate: 9g, Fiber: 1g, Protein: 1g

Tropical Sugar Cookie Bars

• Cookies, **Bars & Bites** •

Oatmeal-Date Cookies

$1/2$ **cup packed light brown sugar**
$1/4$ **cup ($1/2$ stick) margarine, softened**
  1 **whole egg**
  1 **egg white**
  1 **tablespoon frozen apple juice concentrate**
  1 **teaspoon vanilla**
$1 1/2$ **cups all-purpose flour**
  2 **teaspoons baking soda**
$1/4$ **teaspoon salt**
$1 1/2$ **cups quick oats**
$1/2$ **cup chopped dates or raisins**

1. Preheat oven to 350°F. Lightly spray cookie sheets with nonstick cooking spray.

2. Beat brown sugar and margarine in large bowl with electric mixer at medium speed until well blended. Add egg, egg white, apple juice concentrate and vanilla; beat until well blended.

3. Add flour, baking soda and salt; mix well. Stir in oats and dates. Drop dough by teaspoonfuls onto prepared cookie sheets.

4. Bake 8 to 10 minutes or until edges are very lightly browned. (Centers should still be soft.)

5. Cool cookies on cookie sheets 1 minute. Remove to wire racks; cool completely.

Makes 36 cookies

Nutrients per Serving (1 cookie): Calories: 65, Calories from Fat: 27%, Total Fat: 2g, Saturated Fat: <1g, Cholesterol: 6mg, Sodium: 106mg, Carbohydrate: 11g, Fiber: 1g, Protein: 1g

• Cookies, **Bars & Bites** •

Chocolate Cherry Cookies

1 package (9 ounces) chocolate cake mix

3 tablespoons fat-free (skim) milk

$^1\!/_2$ teaspoon almond extract

10 to 12 maraschino cherries, rinsed, drained and cut into halves

2 tablespoons white chocolate chips

$^1\!/_2$ teaspoon canola oil

1. Preheat oven to 350°F. Spray cookie sheets with nonstick cooking spray.

2. Beat cake mix, milk and almond extract in medium bowl with electric mixer at low speed. Increase speed to medium when mixture looks crumbly; beat 2 minutes or until smooth dough forms. (Dough will be very sticky.)

3. Coat hands with cooking spray. Shape dough into 1-inch balls. Place balls 2$^1\!/_2$ inches apart on prepared cookie sheets. Flatten each ball slightly. Place cherry half in center of each cookie.

4. Bake 8 to 9 minutes or until cookies are no longer shiny and tops begin to crack. Remove to wire racks; cool completely.

5. Place white chocolate chips and oil in small microwavable bowl. Microwave on HIGH 30 seconds; stir. Repeat as necessary until chips are melted and mixture is smooth. Drizzle white chocolate glaze over cookies. Let stand until set.

Makes about 24 cookies

Nutrients per Serving (1 cookie): Calories: 54, Calories from Fat: 17%, Total Fat: 1g, Saturated Fat: 1g, Cholesterol: <1mg, Sodium: 79mg, Carbohydrate: 10g, Fiber: <1g, Protein: 1g

Chocolate Cherry Cookies

·Tasty·
Tidbits

Mediterranean Pita Pizzas

2 (8-inch) rounds pita bread
1 teaspoon olive oil
1 cup canned cannellini beans, rinsed and drained
2 teaspoons lemon juice
2 cloves garlic, minced
$\frac{1}{2}$ cup thinly sliced radicchio or escarole lettuce (optional)
$\frac{1}{2}$ cup chopped seeded tomato
$\frac{1}{2}$ cup finely chopped red onion
$\frac{1}{4}$ cup (1 ounce) crumbled feta cheese
2 tablespoons sliced pitted black olives

1. Preheat oven to 450°F. Arrange pitas on baking sheet; brush tops with oil. Bake 6 minutes.

2. Meanwhile, place beans in small bowl; mash lightly with fork. Stir in lemon juice and garlic.

3. Spread bean mixture evenly on pitas to within $\frac{1}{2}$ inch of edges. Top with radicchio, if desired, tomato, onion, feta and olives.

4. Bake 5 minutes or until toppings are thoroughly heated and crust is crisp. Cut into quarters; serve hot. *Makes 8 servings*

Nutrients per Serving (1 wedge): Calories: 98, Calories from Fat: 29%, Total Fat: 3g, Saturated Fat: 1g, Cholesterol: 7mg, Sodium: 282mg, Carbohydrate: 14g, Fiber: 2g, Protein: 4g

Stuffed Baguette

2 medium red bell peppers
1 loaf French bread (about 14 inches long)
¹⁄₄ cup plus 2 tablespoons fat-free Italian dressing, divided
1 small red onion, very thinly sliced
8 large fresh basil leaves
3 ounces Swiss cheese, very thinly sliced

1. Preheat oven to 425°F. Line large baking sheet with foil.

2. To roast bell peppers, cut in half; remove stems, seeds and membranes. Place peppers, cut sides down, on prepared baking sheet. Bake 20 to 25 minutes or until skins are browned.

3. Transfer peppers to paper bag; close bag. Let stand 10 minutes or until peppers are cool enough to handle and skins are loosened. Peel off and discard skins; cut peppers into strips.

4. Trim ends from bread. Cut loaf in half lengthwise. Remove soft insides of loaf and reserve for another use.

5. Brush ¹⁄₄ cup Italian dressing evenly onto cut sides of bread. Arrange pepper strips on bottom half of loaf; top with onion. Brush onion with remaining 2 tablespoons Italian dressing; top with basil and cheese. Replace top half of loaf. Wrap loaf tightly in plastic wrap; refrigerate at least 2 hours.

6. Cut loaf crosswise into 1-inch slices. Secure with toothpicks.

Makes 12 servings

Nutrients per Serving (1 slice): Calories: 98, Calories from Fat: 25%, Total Fat: 3g, Saturated Fat: 1g, Cholesterol: 7mg, Sodium: 239mg, Carbohydrate: 14g, Fiber: 1g, Protein: 4g

Stuffed Baguette

• Tasty **Tidbits** •

New Wave Chicken Salad Wraps

2 cups chopped fresh spinach
1½ cups chopped cooked chicken breast (about 8 ounces uncooked)
1 cup chopped fresh tomatoes
1 cup shredded carrots
1 cup frozen corn, thawed
2 teaspoons garlic-herb seasoning
¼ cup reduced-fat mayonnaise
16 leaves romaine, iceberg or Bibb lettuce

1. Combine all ingredients except lettuce in large bowl; mix well.

2. To serve, spoon ¼ cup chicken mixture onto each lettuce leaf; roll or fold as desired. *Makes 8 servings*

Nutrients per Serving (2 wraps): Calories: 93, Calories from Fat: 31%, Total Fat: 3g, Saturated Fat: <1g, Cholesterol: 23mg, Sodium: 98mg, Carbohydrate: 7g, Fiber: 2g, Protein: 9g

Mini Cheese Burritos

½ cup canned fat-free refried beans
4 (8-inch) fat-free flour tortillas
½ cup chunky salsa
4 (¾-ounce) reduced-fat Cheddar cheese sticks*
Reduced-fat Cheddar cheese block can be substituted. Cut cheese into sticks.

Microwave Directions

1. Spread beans over tortillas, leaving ½ inch border around edges. Spoon salsa over beans.

2. Place cheese stick on one side of each tortilla. Fold edge of tortilla over cheese stick; roll up. Place burritos, seam side down, in microwavable dish.

3. Microwave on HIGH 1 to 2 minutes or until cheese is melted. Let stand 1 to 2 minutes before serving. *Makes 4 servings*

Nutrients per Serving (1 burrito): Calories: 109, Calories from Fat: 31%, Total Fat: 4g, Saturated Fat: 3g, Cholesterol: 10mg, Sodium: 435mg, Carbohydrate: 11g, Fiber: 4g, Protein: 9g

94 calories

Tomato-Herb Soup

1 can (about 14 ounces) no-salt-added diced tomatoes
1 can (about 14 ounces) reduced-sodium chicken broth
1 package (8 ounces) frozen bell pepper stir-fry mixture
1 cup frozen green beans
1/2 cup water
1 tablespoon ketchup
1 to 2 teaspoons dried oregano
1 teaspoon dried basil
1/8 teaspoon red pepper flakes (optional)
1 tablespoon olive oil
1/2 teaspoon salt (optional)

1. Combine tomatoes, broth, bell peppers, green beans, water, ketchup, oregano, basil and red pepper flakes, if desired, in large saucepan. Bring to a boil over high heat. Reduce heat; cover and simmer 20 minutes or until beans are tender.

2. Remove from heat. Stir in oil and salt, if desired.   *Makes 4 servings*

Variation: Substitute chopped fresh bell peppers for the frozen stir-fry mix.

Nutrients per Serving: Calories: 94, Calories from Fat: 28%, Total Fat: 3g, Saturated Fat: <1g, Cholesterol: 0mg, Sodium: 327mg, Carbohydrate: 14g, Fiber: 4g, Protein: 3g

•Tasty **Tidbits**•

Black Bean Quesadillas

Nonstick cooking spray
4 (8-inch) flour tortillas
3/4 cup (3 ounces) shredded reduced-fat Monterey Jack or Cheddar cheese
1/2 cup canned black beans, rinsed and drained
2 green onions, sliced
1/4 cup chopped fresh cilantro
1/2 teaspoon ground cumin
1/2 cup salsa
2 tablespoons plus 2 teaspoons fat-free sour cream
Additional fresh cilantro (optional)

1. Preheat oven to 450°F. Spray large nonstick baking sheet with cooking spray. Place two tortillas on prepared baking sheet; sprinkle each with half of cheese.

2. Combine beans, green onions, cilantro and cumin in small bowl; mix lightly. Spoon bean mixture evenly over cheese; top with remaining tortillas. Spray tops with cooking spray.

3. Bake 10 to 12 minutes or until cheese is melted and tortillas are lightly browned. Cut into quarters; top each tortilla wedge with 1 tablespoon salsa and 1 teaspoon sour cream. Garnish with cilantro. *Makes 8 servings*

Nutrients per Serving (1 wedge with 1 tablespoon salsa and 1 teaspoon sour cream): Calories: 105, Calories from Fat: 34%, Total Fat: 4g, Saturated Fat: 1g, Cholesterol: 8mg, Sodium: 259mg, Carbohydrate: 13g, Fiber: 1g, Protein: 7g

Tip The possibilities for quesadilla fillings are endless. Try veggies such as bell peppers, mushrooms, zucchini or squash. Any cheese would work well, even a nontraditional one like goat cheese. For heartier quesadillas, add chopped cooked chicken, beef or pork.

Black Bean Quesadilla

Peppered Shrimp Skewers

⅓ **cup teriyaki sauce**

⅓ **cup ketchup**

2 **tablespoons dry sherry or water**

2 **tablespoons reduced-fat peanut butter**

1 **teaspoon hot pepper sauce**

¼ **teaspoon ground ginger**

2 **large yellow bell peppers**

32 **large raw shrimp (about 1½ pounds), peeled and deveined, with tails on**

32 **fresh sugar snap peas, trimmed**

1. Soak 16 (12-inch) wooden skewers in water at least 20 minutes before assembling kabobs.

2. Preheat broiler. Spray broiler pan with nonstick cooking spray.

3. Combine teriyaki sauce, ketchup, sherry, peanut butter, pepper sauce and ginger in small saucepan. Bring to a boil, stirring constantly. Reduce heat to low; simmer 1 minute. Remove from heat.

4. Cut each bell pepper lengthwise into four quarters; remove stems and seeds. Cut each quarter crosswise into four equal pieces. Thread two shrimp, two bell pepper pieces and two sugar snap peas onto each skewer; place on prepared pan. Brush with teriyaki sauce mixture.

5. Broil skewers 4 inches from heat 3 minutes; turn. Brush with teriyaki sauce mixture; broil 2 minutes or until shrimp turn pink and opaque. Discard any remaining teriyaki sauce mixture. *Makes 16 servings*

Nutrients per Serving (1 skewer): Calories: 79, Calories from Fat: 23%, Total Fat: 2g, Saturated Fat: <1g, Cholesterol: 66mg, Sodium: 245mg, Carbohydrate: 7g, Fiber: 1g, Protein: 10g

Peppered Shrimp Skewer

Mini Chickpea Cakes

1 can (about 15 ounces) chickpeas, rinsed and drained
1 cup shredded carrots
$^1/_3$ cup seasoned dry bread crumbs
$^1/_4$ cup reduced-fat creamy Italian salad dressing, plus additional for dipping
1 egg

1. Preheat oven to 375°F. Spray baking sheets with nonstick cooking spray.

2. Coarsely mash chickpeas in medium bowl with potato masher. Stir in carrots, bread crumbs, $^1/_4$ cup salad dressing and egg; mix well.

3. Shape chickpea mixture into 24 patties, using about 1 tablespoon mixture for each. Place on prepared baking sheets.

4. Bake 15 to 18 minutes or until chickpea cakes are lightly browned on both sides, turning halfway through baking time. Serve warm with additional salad dressing for dipping, if desired. *Makes 8 servings*

Nutrients per Serving (3 cakes without additional dressing): Calories: 102, Calories from Fat: 17%, Total Fat: 2g, Saturated Fat: 1g, Cholesterol: 27mg, Sodium: 314mg, Carbohydrate: 17g, Fiber: 3g, Protein: 4g

Crostini with Lemony Pesto

1 (4-ounce) French baguette
3 tablespoons pesto
$^1/_2$ teaspoon lemon juice
$^1/_2$ cup chopped plum tomato

1. Preheat oven to 350°F.

2. Cut baguette crosswise into 16 slices; arrange on baking sheet. Bake 11 to 12 minutes or until bread begins to brown. Cool completely.

3. Combine pesto and lemon juice in small bowl; stir until well blended. Spread each bread slice with $^1/_2$ teaspoon pesto mixture. Top with tomato. Serve immediately. *Makes 16 servings*

Nutrients per Serving (1 crostino): Calories: 33, Calories from Fat: 39%, Total Fat: 1g, Saturated Fat: <1g, Cholesterol: <1mg, Sodium: 64mg, Carbohydrate: 4g, Fiber: <1g, Protein: 1g

Mini Chickpea Cakes

Caribbean Chutney Kabobs

$1/2$ **medium pineapple**

$3/4$ **pound boneless skinless chicken breasts, cut into 1-inch pieces**

1 **medium red bell pepper, cut into 1-inch pieces**

$1/2$ **cup mango chutney**

2 **tablespoons orange juice or pineapple juice**

1 **teaspoon vanilla**

$1/4$ **teaspoon ground nutmeg**

1. Soak 20 (4-inch) wooden skewers in water at least 20 minutes before assembling kabobs.

2. Peel and core pineapple. Cut pineapple into 1-inch chunks. Alternately thread chicken, pineapple and bell pepper onto skewers. Place in shallow baking dish.

3. Combine chutney, orange juice, vanilla and nutmeg in small bowl; mix well. Pour over kabobs. Cover and refrigerate up to 4 hours.

4. Preheat broiler. Spray broiler pan with nonstick cooking spray. Place kabobs on prepared pan; discard marinade.

5. Broil kabobs 6 to 8 inches from heat 4 to 5 minutes per side or until chicken is cooked through. *Makes 10 servings*

Nutrients per Serving (2 kabobs): Calories: 108, Calories from Fat: 10%, Total Fat: 1g, Saturated Fat: <1g, Cholesterol: 21mg, Sodium: 22mg, Carbohydrate: 16g, Fiber: 2g, Protein: 8g

Caribbean Chutney Kabobs

87 calories

Veggie Pizza Pitas

2 rounds whole wheat pita bread, cut in half horizontally (to make 4 rounds)
$1/4$ cup pizza sauce
1 teaspoon dried basil
$1/8$ teaspoon red pepper flakes (optional)
1 cup sliced mushrooms
$1/2$ cup thinly sliced green bell pepper
$1/2$ cup thinly sliced red onion
$1/2$ cup (2 ounces) shredded mozzarella cheese
2 teaspoons grated Parmesan cheese

1. Preheat oven to 475°F.

2. Arrange pitas, rough sides up, in single layer on large nonstick baking sheet. Spread 1 tablespoon pizza sauce evenly over each round to within $1/4$ inch of edge. Sprinkle with basil and red pepper flakes, if desired. Top with mushrooms, bell pepper and onion. Sprinkle with mozzarella.

3. Bake 5 minutes or until cheese is melted. Sprinkle $1/2$ teaspoon Parmesan over each pizza. *Makes 4 servings*

Nutrients per Serving (1 pizza): Calories: 87, Calories from Fat: 21%, Total Fat: 2g, Saturated Fat: <1g, Cholesterol: 4mg, Sodium: 293mg, Carbohydrate: 12g, Fiber: 2g, Protein: 7g

Veggie Pizza Pita

• Tasty **Tidbits** •

Asian Vegetable Rolls with Soy-Lime Dipping Sauce

1/4 **cup reduced-sodium soy sauce**

 2 **tablespoons lime juice**

 1 **clove garlic, crushed**

 1 **teaspoon honey**

1/2 **teaspoon finely chopped fresh ginger**

1/4 **teaspoon dark sesame oil**

1/8 **to** 1/4 **teaspoon red pepper flakes**

1/2 **cup grated cucumber**

1/3 **cup grated carrot**

1/4 **cup sliced yellow bell pepper (1 inch long)**

 2 **tablespoons thinly sliced green onion**

18 **small lettuce leaves**

 Sesame seeds (optional)

1. Combine soy sauce, lime juice, garlic, honey, ginger, oil and red pepper flakes in small bowl.

2. Combine cucumber, carrot, bell pepper and green onion in medium bowl. Stir in 1 tablespoon soy sauce mixture.

3. Place about 1 tablespoon vegetable mixture on each lettuce leaf. Roll up leaves; sprinkle with sesame seeds, if desired. Serve with remaining sauce for dipping.

Makes 6 servings

Nutrients per Serving (3 rolls with 1 tablespoon dipping sauce): Calories: 25, Calories from Fat: 11%, Total Fat: <1g, Saturated Fat: <1g, Cholesterol: 0mg, Sodium: 343mg, Carbohydrate: 5g, Fiber: 1g, Protein: 1g

Asian Vegetable Rolls with Soy-Lime Dipping Sauce

Open-Faced Egg Salad Sandwiches

6 hard-cooked eggs
3 tablespoons reduced-fat mayonnaise
¹/₂ cup finely chopped green onions
1¹/₂ tablespoons sweet pickle relish
¹/₄ to ¹/₂ teaspoon celery seed
¹/₄ teaspoon salt
¹/₈ teaspoon black pepper
4 slices reduced-calorie, high-fiber bread
2 cups packed spring greens

1. Separate egg yolks from whites; discard 4 yolks or reserve for another use.

2. Combine remaining 2 egg yolks and mayonnaise in medium bowl; mix well. Finely chop egg whites and add to mixture. Stir in green onions, pickle relish, celery seed, salt and pepper; mix well.

3. Top each bread slice evenly with greens and egg salad. *Makes 4 servings*

Nutrients per Serving: Calories: 104, Calories from Fat: 23%, Total Fat: 3g, Saturated Fat: <1g, Cholesterol: 104mg, Sodium: 400mg, Carbohydrate: 14g, Fiber: 6g, Protein: 9g

 To prepare hard-cooked eggs, place the eggs in a single layer in a saucepan. Add cold water to cover the eggs by 1 inch; cover and bring to a boil over high heat. Remove the pan from the heat and let stand 15 minutes. Immediately pour off the water, cover the eggs with cold water and let stand until the eggs have cooled.

Open-Faced Egg Salad Sandwich

• Tasty **Tidbits** •

Wild Wedges

2 (8-inch) fat-free flour tortillas
Nonstick cooking spray
¹/₃ cup shredded reduced-fat Cheddar cheese
¹/₃ cup chopped cooked chicken or turkey
1 green onion, thinly sliced
2 tablespoons mild thick and chunky salsa

1. Heat large nonstick skillet over medium heat.

2. Spray one side of one tortilla with cooking spray; place in skillet sprayed side down. Top with cheese, chicken, green onion and salsa. Top with remaining tortilla; spray with cooking spray.

3. Cook 2 to 3 minutes per side or until golden brown and cheese is melted. Cut into 8 wedges. *Makes 4 servings*

Variation: For bean quesadillas, omit the chicken and spread ¹/₃ cup canned fat-free refried beans over one of the tortillas.

Nutrients per Serving (2 wedges): Calories: 82, Calories from Fat: 25%, Total Fat: 2g, Saturated Fat: 1g, Cholesterol: 13mg, Sodium: 224mg, Carbohydrate: 8g, Fiber: 3g, Protein: 7g

Tip Rotisserie chicken is one of the most popular convenience products at the supermarket—with good reason. One whole cooked chicken will yield about 2¹/₂ cups chopped chicken, enough to use in several snacks or meals throughout the week.

Angelic Deviled Eggs

6 eggs
¼ cup low-fat (1%) cottage cheese
3 tablespoons fat-free ranch dressing
2 teaspoons Dijon mustard
2 tablespoons minced fresh chives or dill
1 tablespoon diced well-drained pimiento or roasted red pepper

1. Place eggs in medium saucepan; add enough water to cover by 1 inch. Cover and bring to a boil over high heat. Remove from heat; let stand 15 minutes. Drain. Add cold water to eggs in saucepan; let stand until eggs are cool. Drain and peel.

2. Cut eggs in half lengthwise. Remove yolks, reserving 3 yolk halves. Discard remaining yolks or reserve for another use. Place egg whites, cut sides up, on serving plate; cover with plastic wrap. Refrigerate while preparing filling.

3. Combine cottage cheese, dressing, mustard and reserved yolk halves in small bowl; mash with fork until well blended. Stir in chives and pimiento. Spoon into egg whites. Cover and refrigerate at least 1 hour. *Makes 12 servings*

Nutrients per Serving (1 egg half): Calories: 44, Calories from Fat: 52%, Total Fat: 3g, Saturated Fat: <1g, Cholesterol: 27mg, Sodium: 96mg, Carbohydrate: 1g, Fiber: 1g, Protein: 4g

Angelic Deviled Eggs

·Munchies·
& Things

Savory Zucchini Sticks

Nonstick cooking spray
3 tablespoons seasoned dry bread crumbs
2 tablespoons grated Parmesan cheese
1 egg white
1 teaspoon reduced-fat (2%) milk
2 small zucchini (about 4 ounces each), cut lengthwise into quarters
1/3 cup pasta sauce, warmed

1. Preheat oven to 400°F. Spray baking sheet with cooking spray.

2. Combine bread crumbs and Parmesan in shallow dish. Combine egg white and milk in another shallow dish; beat with fork until well blended.

3. Dip each zucchini stick first into crumb mixture, then into egg white mixture, letting excess drip back into dish. Roll again in crumb mixture to coat. Place zucchini sticks on prepared baking sheet; spray with cooking spray.

4. Bake 15 to 18 minutes or until golden brown. Serve with pasta sauce.

Makes 4 servings

Nutrients per Serving (2 sticks with 4 teaspoons pasta sauce): Calories: 69, Calories from Fat: 26%, Total Fat: 2g, Saturated Fat: 1g, Cholesterol: 6mg, Sodium: 329mg, Carbohydrate: 9g, Fiber: 1g, Protein: 4g

• Munchies **& Things** •

Taco Popcorn Olé

9 cups air-popped popcorn
   Butter-flavored cooking spray
1 teaspoon chili powder
¹/₂ teaspoon salt
¹/₂ teaspoon garlic powder
¹/₈ teaspoon ground red pepper (optional)

1. Preheat oven to 350°F. Line 15×10×1-inch jelly-roll pan with foil.

2. Place popcorn in single layer on prepared pan. Spray lightly with cooking spray.

3. Combine chili powder, salt, garlic powder and red pepper, if desired, in small bowl. Sprinkle spice mixture over popcorn; mix lightly to coat.

4. Bake 5 minutes or until heated through, stirring gently after 3 minutes. Spread popcorn in single layer on large sheet of foil to cool.   *Makes 6 servings*

Tip: Store popcorn in tightly covered container at room temperature up to 4 days.

Nutrients per Serving (1¹/₂ cups): Calories: 48, Calories from Fat: 18%, Total Fat: 1g, Saturated Fat: <1g, Cholesterol: 0mg, Sodium: 199mg, Carbohydrate: 10g, Fiber: 2g, Protein: 2g

Tip For a spicier version, substitute a hot Mexican-style chili powder or a chipotle chili powder for the regular chili powder, or add the ground red pepper.

• Munchies & Things •

Spiced Sesame Wonton Crisps

20 (3-inch) wonton wrappers, cut in half
1 tablespoon water
2 teaspoons olive oil
$1/2$ teaspoon paprika
$1/2$ teaspoon ground cumin or chili powder
$1/4$ teaspoon dry mustard
1 tablespoon sesame seeds

1. Preheat oven to 375°F. Spray baking sheets with nonstick cooking spray.

2. Cut each halved wonton wrapper into 2 strips; place in single layer on prepared baking sheets.

3. Combine water, oil, paprika, cumin and mustard in small bowl; mix well. Brush oil mixture evenly onto wonton strips; sprinkle with sesame seeds.

4. Bake 6 to 8 minutes or until lightly browned. Remove to wire racks; cool completely. *Makes 8 servings*

Nutrients per Serving (10 crisps): Calories: 75, Calories from Fat: 24%, Total Fat: 2g, Saturated Fat: <1g, Cholesterol: 3mg, Sodium: 116mg, Carbohydrate: 12g, Fiber: <1g, Protein: 2g

Creamy Dill Cheese Spread

2 tablespoons reduced-fat cream cheese with herbs and garlic
1 tablespoon reduced-fat mayonnaise
1 tablespoon reduced-fat sour cream
1 to 2 teaspoons chopped fresh dill
$1/8$ teaspoon salt (optional)
24 garlic-flavored melba rounds

1. Combine cream cheese, mayonnaise, sour cream, dill and salt, if desired, in small bowl. Cover with plastic wrap; refrigerate 1 hour.

2. To serve, top each melba round with $1/2$ teaspoon spread. *Makes 4 servings*

Nutrients per Serving (6 topped rounds): Calories: 95, Calories from Fat: 28%, Total Fat: 3g, Saturated Fat: 1g, Cholesterol: 6mg, Sodium: 170mg, Carbohydrate: 14g, Fiber: 1g, Protein: 2g

Spiced Sesame Wonton Crisps

Munchies & Things

Herbed Potato Chips

Nonstick cooking spray

2 unpeeled medium red potatoes (about $\frac{1}{2}$ pound), very thinly sliced

1 tablespoon olive oil

2 tablespoons minced fresh dill, thyme or rosemary leaves *or* 2 teaspoons dried dill weed, thyme or rosemary

$\frac{1}{4}$ teaspoon garlic salt

$\frac{1}{8}$ teaspoon black pepper

$1\frac{1}{4}$ cups fat-free sour cream

1. Preheat oven to 450°F. Spray baking sheets with cooking spray. Pat potatoes dry with paper towels. Arrange in single layer on prepared baking sheets; spray with cooking spray.

2. Bake 10 minutes; turn slices. Brush with oil. Combine dill, garlic salt and pepper in small bowl; sprinkle evenly on potatoes. Bake 5 to 10 minutes or until golden brown. Cool on baking sheets. Serve with sour cream. *Makes 6 servings*

Nutrients per Serving (10 chips with about 3 tablespoons sour cream): Calories: 106, Calories from Fat: 17%, Total Fat: 2g, Saturated Fat: <1g, Cholesterol: 8mg, Sodium: 84mg, Carbohydrate: 16g, Fiber: 1g, Protein: 4g

Rosemary-Scented Nut Mix

2 tablespoons unsalted butter

2 cups pecan halves

1 cup unsalted macadamia nuts

1 cup walnuts

1 teaspoon dried rosemary

$\frac{1}{2}$ teaspoon salt

$\frac{1}{4}$ teaspoon red pepper flakes

1. Preheat oven to 300°F. Melt butter in large saucepan over low heat. Add pecans, macadamia nuts and walnuts; mix well. Add rosemary, salt and red pepper flakes; cook and stir about 1 minute.

2. Spread mixture onto ungreased nonstick baking sheet. Bake 15 minutes, stirring occasionally. Cool completely on baking sheet on wire rack. *Makes 32 servings*

Nutrients per Serving (2 tablespoons): Calories: 108, Calories from Fat: 92%, Total Fat: 11g, Saturated Fat: 2g, Cholesterol: 2mg, Sodium: 37mg, Carbohydrate: 2g, Fiber: 1g, Protein: 2g

Herbed Potato Chips

• Munchies & Things •

Southwest Snack Mix

4 cups unsweetened corn cereal squares
2 cups unsalted pretzels
$^1/_2$ cup unsalted pumpkin or squash seeds
1$^1/_2$ teaspoons chili powder
1 teaspoon minced fresh cilantro or parsley
$^1/_2$ teaspoon garlic powder
$^1/_2$ teaspoon onion powder
1 egg white
2 tablespoons olive oil
2 tablespoons lime juice

1. Preheat oven to 300°F. Spray baking sheet with nonstick cooking spray.

2. Combine cereal, pretzels and pumpkin seeds in large bowl. Combine chili powder, cilantro, garlic powder and onion powder in small bowl.

3. Whisk egg white, oil and lime juice in separate small bowl until well blended. Pour over cereal mixture; toss to coat. Add seasoning mixture; mix lightly to coat. Transfer to prepared baking sheet.

4. Bake 45 minutes, stirring every 15 minutes. Cool completely. Store in airtight container.   *Makes about 12 servings*

Variation: Substitute $^1/_2$ cup unsalted peanuts for pumpkin seeds.

Nutrients per Serving ($^1/_2$ cup): Calories: 93, Calories from Fat: 28%, Total Fat: 3g, Saturated Fat: <1g, Cholesterol: 0mg, Sodium: 114mg, Carbohydrate: 15g, Fiber: 1g, Protein: 2g

Southwest Snack Mix

• Munchies & Things •

Great Zukes Pizza Bites

1 medium zucchini
3 tablespoons pizza sauce
2 tablespoons tomato paste
¼ teaspoon dried oregano
¾ cup (3 ounces) shredded mozzarella cheese
¼ cup shredded Parmesan cheese
8 slices pitted black olives
8 slices pepperoni

1. Preheat broiler; set rack 4 inches from heat.

2. Trim off and discard ends of zucchini. Cut zucchini into 16 (¼-inch-thick) diagonal slices. Place on nonstick baking sheet.

3. Combine pizza sauce, tomato paste and oregano in small bowl; mix well. Spread scant teaspoon sauce over each zucchini slice. Combine cheeses in small bowl. Top each zucchini slice with 1 tablespoon cheese mixture, pressing down into sauce. Place one olive slice on each of eight pizza bites. Place one folded pepperoni slice on each remaining pizza bite.

4. Broil 3 minutes or until cheese is melted. Serve immediately.   *Makes 8 servings*

....

Nutrients per Serving (2 bites): Calories: 75, Calories from Fat: 60%, Total Fat: 5g, Saturated Fat: 2g, Cholesterol: 10mg, Sodium: 288mg, Carbohydrate: 3g, Fiber: 1g, Protein: 5g

• Munchies **& Things** •

Peppy Snack Mix

3 (3-inch) plain rice cakes, broken into bite-size pieces
1½ cups bite-size frosted shredded wheat cereal
¾ cup pretzel sticks, halved
3 tablespoons reduced-fat margarine, melted
2 teaspoons reduced-sodium Worcestershire sauce
¾ teaspoon chili powder
⅛ to ¼ teaspoon ground red pepper

1. Preheat oven to 300°F. Combine rice cake pieces, cereal and pretzels in 13×9-inch baking pan.

2. Combine margarine, Worcestershire sauce, chili powder and red pepper in small bowl. Drizzle over cereal mixture; toss to combine.

3. Bake 20 minutes, stirring after 10 minutes. *Makes 8 servings*

Nutrients per Serving (½ cup): Calories: 94, Calories from Fat: 23%, Total Fat: 2g, Saturated Fat: <1g, Cholesterol: 0mg, Sodium: 125mg, Carbohydrate: 16g, Fiber: <1g, Protein: 2g

Cheesy Barbecued Bean Dip

93
calories

½ cup canned vegetarian baked beans
3 tablespoons pasteurized process cheese product
2 tablespoons regular or hickory smoke barbecue sauce
2 large carrots, cut into diagonal slices
1 medium red or green bell pepper, cut into slices

Microwave Directions

1. Place beans in small microwavable bowl; mash slightly with fork. Stir in process cheese product and barbecue sauce. Cover with vented plastic wrap.

2. Microwave on HIGH 1 minute; stir. Microwave 30 seconds or until hot. Serve with carrot and bell pepper slices. *Makes 4 servings*

Nutrients per Serving: Calories: 93, Calories from Fat: 25%, Total Fat: 3g, Saturated Fat: 1g, Cholesterol: 10mg, Sodium: 355mg, Carbohydrate: 15g, Fiber: 4g, Protein: 4g

Peppy Snack Mix

Munchies & Things

Super Nachos

12 large baked reduced-fat tortilla chips (about 1¹⁄₂ ounces)
¹⁄₂ cup (2 ounces) shredded reduced-fat Cheddar cheese
¹⁄₄ cup fat-free refried beans
2 tablespoons chunky salsa
Fresh cilantro (optional)

Microwave Directions

1. Arrange chips in single layer on large microwavable plate. Sprinkle cheese evenly over chips.

2. Spoon 1 teaspoon beans over each chip; top with ¹⁄₂ teaspoon salsa.

3. Microwave on MEDIUM (50%) 2 to 3 minutes or until cheese is melted. Garnish with cilantro.

Makes 4 servings

Conventional Directions: Preheat oven to 350°F. Line baking sheet with foil. Assemble nachos on prepared baking sheet as directed above. Bake 10 to 12 minutes or until cheese is melted.

Tip: For a single serving of nachos, arrange 3 large tortilla chips on a microwavable plate. Top chips with 2 tablespoons cheese, 1 tablespoon refried beans and about ¹⁄₂ tablespoon salsa. Microwave on MEDIUM (50%) 1 to 1¹⁄₂ minutes or until cheese is melted.

Nutrients per Serving (3 nachos): Calories: 82, Calories from Fat: 44%, Total Fat: 4g, Saturated Fat: 2g, Cholesterol: 10mg, Sodium: 263mg, Carbohydrate: 6g, Fiber: 1g, Protein: 4g

•Munchies **&** Things•

Savory Pita Chips

2 rounds whole wheat pita bread
Olive oil cooking spray
3 tablespoons grated Parmesan cheese
1 teaspoon dried basil
$1/4$ teaspoon garlic powder

1. Preheat oven to 350°F. Line baking sheet with foil.

2. Cut each pita in half horizontally to make two rounds. Cut each round into six wedges.

3. Place wedges, rough side down, on prepared baking sheet; spray lightly with cooking spray. Turn wedges; spray again.

4. Combine Parmesan, basil and garlic powder in small bowl; sprinkle evenly over pita wedges.

5. Bake 12 to 14 minutes or until golden brown. Cool completely.

Makes 4 servings

Cinnamon Crisps: Substitute butter-flavored cooking spray for olive oil-flavored cooking spray, and 1 tablespoon sugar mixed with $1/4$ teaspoon ground cinnamon for Parmesan cheese, basil and garlic powder.

Nutrients per Serving (6 chips): Calories: 108, Calories from Fat: 18%, Total Fat: 2g, Saturated Fat: 1g, Cholesterol: 4mg, Sodium: 257mg, Carbohydrate: 18g, Fiber: 2g, Protein: 5g

Savory Pita Chips

26 calories

BLT Cukes

½ cup finely chopped lettuce
½ cup finely chopped baby spinach
3 slices bacon, crisp-cooked and crumbled
¼ cup finely diced tomato
1 tablespoon plus 1½ teaspoons fat-free mayonnaise
¼ teaspoon black pepper
⅛ teaspoon salt
1 large cucumber
Minced fresh parsley or green onion (optional)

1. Combine lettuce, spinach, bacon, tomato, mayonnaise, pepper and salt in medium bowl; mix well.

2. Peel cucumber; trim off ends and cut in half lengthwise. Use spoon to scoop out seeds; discard seeds.

3. Divide bacon mixture between cucumber halves, mounding in center. Garnish with parsley. Cut into 2-inch pieces.   *Makes 10 servings*

Tip: Make these snacks when cucumbers are plentiful and large enough to easily hollow out with a spoon. These snacks can be made, covered and refrigerated up to 12 hours ahead of time.

Nutrients per Serving (1 piece): Calories: 26, Calories from Fat: 69%, Total Fat: 2g, Saturated Fat: <1g, Cholesterol: 3mg, Sodium: 72mg, Carbohydrate: 2g, Fiber: <1g, Protein: 2g

·200 Calorie·
Contents

·Cakes &·
Cheesecakes

Zucchini Spice Bundt Cake

    1 package (about 18 ounces) spice or carrot cake mix
    1 cup water
 ³/₄ cup cholesterol-free egg substitute
    2 tablespoons canola oil
    1 medium zucchini, shredded
    3 tablespoons chopped walnuts, toasted*
 ³/₄ teaspoon vanilla
 ¹/₄ cup powdered sugar
    1 to 2 teaspoons fat-free (skim) milk

*To toast walnuts, spread in single layer on baking sheet. Bake in preheated 350°F oven 5 to 7 minutes or until golden brown, stirring frequently.

1. Preheat oven to 325°F. Spray 12-cup bundt pan with nonstick cooking spray.

2. Combine cake mix, water, egg substitute and oil in large bowl; mix according to package directions. Stir in zucchini, walnuts and vanilla until well blended. Pour into prepared pan.

3. Bake 40 to 45 minutes or until toothpick inserted near center comes out almost clean. Cool in pan on wire rack 10 minutes. Invert onto wire rack; cool completely.

4. For glaze, combine powdered sugar and milk in small bowl; stir until smooth. Drizzle glaze over cake. *Makes 18 servings*

Nutrients per Serving: Calories: 154, Calories from Fat: 28%, Total Fat: 5g, Saturated Fat: 1g, Cholesterol: 0mg, Sodium: 205mg, Carbohydrate: 25g, Fiber: <1g, Protein: 2g

• Cakes & **Cheesecakes** •

Key Lime Cheesecake with Strawberries and Fresh Mint

12 whole low-fat honey graham crackers, broken into small pieces
2 tablespoons reduced-fat margarine
2 packages (8 ounces each) reduced-fat cream cheese, softened
1 package (8 ounces) fat-free cream cheese, softened
1 container (6 ounces) plain nonfat yogurt
$^2/_3$ cup powdered sugar
8 packets sugar substitute *or* equivalent of $^1/_3$ cup sugar, divided
2 teaspoons grated lime peel
$^1/_4$ cup lime juice
$1^1/_2$ teaspoons vanilla
3 cups fresh strawberries, quartered
2 tablespoons finely chopped fresh mint leaves

1. Preheat oven to 350°F. Spray 9-inch springform pan with nonstick cooking spray.

2. Place cracker pieces and margarine in food processor; process with on/off pulses until coarse crumbs form. Gently press crumb mixture onto bottom and $^1/_2$ inch up side of prepared pan. Bake 8 to 10 minutes or until lightly browned; cool completely on wire rack.

3. Beat cream cheese, yogurt, powdered sugar, 6 packets sugar substitute, lime peel, lime juice and vanilla in large bowl with electric mixer at high speed until smooth. Pour into cooled crust. Cover and freeze 2 hours or refrigerate overnight.

4. Combine strawberries, remaining 2 packets sugar substitute and mint in medium bowl 30 minutes before serving. Just before serving, spoon strawberry mixture over cheesecake. *Makes 12 servings*

Nutrients per Serving: Calories: 176, Calories from Fat: 35%, Total Fat: 7g, Saturated Fat: 5g, Cholesterol: 20mg, Sodium: 341mg, Carbohydrate: 18g, Fiber: 1g, Protein: 8g

Key Lime Cheesecake with Strawberries and Fresh Mint

• Cakes & Cheesecakes •

Enlightened Oatmeal Cake

Cake

1¼ cups boiling water
1 cup old-fashioned oats
1 cup sugar substitute*
¾ cup packed light brown sugar
¼ cup canola oil
1 egg
2 egg whites
1 teaspoon vanilla
1½ cups all-purpose flour
1 teaspoon baking soda
¾ teaspoon ground cinnamon
½ teaspoon salt
¼ teaspoon ground nutmeg

Frosting

½ cup packed light brown sugar
½ cup chopped nuts
⅓ cup shredded coconut
3 tablespoons diet margarine, softened
3 tablespoons fat-free (skim) milk

This recipe was tested with sucralose-based sugar substitute.

1. Preheat oven to 350°F. Spray 11×7 inch baking pan with nonstick cooking spray. Pour boiling water over oats in heatproof bowl. Cover and let stand 20 minutes.

2. Beat sugar substitute, ¾ cup brown sugar and oil in large bowl with electric mixer at low speed 30 seconds or until well blended. Add egg, egg whites and vanilla; beat until smooth. Mix in oats.

3. Sift together flour, baking soda, cinnamon, salt and nutmeg. Slowly add to oat mixture; beat at low speed until well blended. Pour into prepared pan. Bake 32 to 34 minutes or until toothpick inserted in center comes out clean.

4. Preheat broiler. Stir frosting ingredients in medium bowl until well blended. Spoon evenly over cake in pan. Broil cake 4 inches from heat 2 minutes or until golden.

Makes 16 servings

Nutrients per Serving: Calories: 205, Calories from Fat: 35%, Total Fat: 8g, Saturated Fat: 1g, Cholesterol: 13mg, Sodium: 185mg, Carbohydrate: 32g, Fiber: 1g, Protein: 3g

• Cakes & **Cheesecakes** •

Cocoa-Swirl Cheesecake

6 whole graham crackers, finely crushed
1 tablespoon granulated sugar
3 tablespoons unsweetened cocoa powder, divided
3 tablespoons reduced-fat soft spread made with yogurt, melted
2¹/₂ cups reduced-fat ricotta cheese
¹/₂ cup sucralose-sugar blend
4 ounces reduced-fat cream cheese, softened
1 cup cholesterol-free egg substitute
2 teaspoons vanilla
Fresh raspberries and mint leaves (optional)

1. Preheat oven to 325°F. Combine cracker crumbs, granulated sugar and 1 tablespoon cocoa in medium bowl. Add spread; stir with fork until moistened. Press crumb mixture onto bottom of 9-inch springform pan. Bake 10 to 12 minutes; cool completely on wire rack. Wrap bottom of pan with foil.

2. Place ricotta in food processor; process several minutes or until very smooth. Add sucralose-sugar blend and cream cheese; process 1 minute or until blended. Gradually add egg substitute and vanilla until blended. Reserve ²/₃ cup batter in small bowl. Pour remaining batter into cooled crust.

3. Stir remaining 2 tablespoons cocoa into reserved batter until well blended. Drop spoonfuls of chocolate batter evenly onto batter in pan; swirl with knife to marbleize.

4. Bake 65 to 70 minutes or just until set in center. Remove to wire rack; run small spatula around edge of cheesecake. Cool completely. Remove side of pan. Refrigerate cheesecake at least 4 hours or overnight.

5. Garnish with fresh raspberries and mint.   *Makes 8 servings*

Nutrients per Serving: Calories: 200, Calories from Fat: 27%, Total Fat: 6g, Saturated Fat: 2g, Cholesterol: 15mg, Sodium: 260mg, Carbohydrate: 18g, Fiber: 1g, Protein: 18g

• Cakes & Cheesecakes •

Carrot Cake with Cream Cheese Glaze

Cake

2 cups cake flour

2 teaspoons ground cinnamon

1 teaspoon baking powder

1 teaspoon baking soda

1 teaspoon salt

¾ cup sugar substitute*

¾ cup packed brown sugar

¼ cup vegetable oil

1 cup cholesterol-free egg substitute

½ cup reduced-fat sour cream

3 cups grated carrots

Glaze

4 ounces fat-free cream cheese, softened

¼ cup reduced-fat sour cream

1 tablespoon fat-free (skim) milk

1 teaspoon vanilla

½ cup powdered sugar

This recipe was tested with sucralose-based sugar substitute.

1. Preheat oven to 350°F. Spray 12-cup bundt pan with nonstick cooking spray. Combine flour, cinnamon, baking powder, baking soda and salt in medium bowl.

2. Beat sugar substitute, brown sugar and oil in large bowl with electric mixer at medium speed. Beat in egg substitute and sour cream. Slowly add flour mixture, beating at low speed just until blended. Stir in carrots. Pour into prepared pan.

3. Bake about 50 minutes or until toothpick inserted near center comes out clean. Cool in pan on wire rack 10 minutes. Invert onto wire rack; cool completely.

4. For glaze, whisk cream cheese, sour cream, milk and vanilla in small bowl until smooth. Whisk in powdered sugar. If glaze is too thick, add water, 1 tablespoon at a time. Spoon glaze over cake.

Makes 16 servings

Nutrients per Serving: Calories: 176, Calories from Fat: 26%, Total Fat: 5g, Saturated Fat: 1g, Cholesterol: 5mg, Sodium: 357mg, Carbohydrate: 28g, Fiber: 1g, Protein: 5g

• Cakes & Cheesecakes •

Chocolate Chip Angel Food Cake Kabobs with Strawberry Sauce

1 package (16 ounces) angel food cake mix
1/3 cup mini chocolate chips
24 small fresh strawberries
   Strawberry Sauce (recipe follows)

1. Preheat oven to 350°F. Prepare cake mix according to package directions, adding chocolate chips to batter. Gently spoon batter into three 8 1/2 × 4 1/2-inch loaf pans.

2. Bake on center rack of oven 28 minutes or until high and golden brown. Cool cakes completely in pans on wire racks. Remove from pans; wrap and freeze two cakes for another use. Cut third cake into six slices; gently tear or cut each slice into four pieces.

3. Starting with cake, alternate three cake pieces and three strawberries on each of eight wooden skewers. Serve with Strawberry Sauce.   *Makes 8 servings*

Strawberry Sauce

1 cup sliced fresh strawberries
1 tablespoon sugar
1 teaspoon lemon juice
1/4 cup water
1 teaspoon cornstarch

Mix strawberries, sugar and lemon juice in small saucepan. Blend water and cornstarch in small bowl until smooth; stir into strawberry mixture. Bring to a boil over high heat. Reduce heat to low; simmer, stirring constantly, 1 minute or until mixture thickens. Purée mixture in blender until smooth, if desired.   *Makes 1 cup*

Nutrients per Serving (1 skewer with 2 tablespoons sauce): Calories: 130, Calories from Fat: 10%, Total Fat: 2g, Saturated Fat: 1g, Cholesterol: 0mg, Sodium: 140mg, Carbohydrate: 27g, Fiber: 2g, Protein: 2g

Chocolate Chip Angel Food Cake Kabob with Strawberry Sauce

Italian Cheesecake

9 whole graham crackers, plus additional pieces for garnish
$1/3$ cup packed brown sugar
3 tablespoons unsalted butter, melted
2 packages (8 ounces each) fat-free cream cheese, softened
$1^1/2$ cups sugar substitute*
1 container (15 ounces) fat-free ricotta cheese
2 eggs
$1/2$ cup cholesterol-free egg substitute
3 tablespoons cornstarch
3 tablespoons all-purpose flour
1 teaspoon vanilla
2 cups reduced-fat sour cream
Fresh strawberries (optional)
Fresh mint leaves (optional)

*This recipe was tested with sucralose-based sugar substitute.

1. Spray 9-inch springform pan or deep-dish pie pan with nonstick cooking spray.

2. Place graham crackers in resealable food storage bag; crush into fine crumbs with rolling pin. Mix crumbs and brown sugar in small bowl. Stir in butter until crumbs are moistened. Press crumb mixture onto bottom and 1 inch up side of prepared pan. Refrigerate crust while preparing filling.

3. Preheat oven to 300°F. Beat cream cheese and sugar substitute in large bowl with electric mixer at medium speed until smooth. Add ricotta; beat until blended. Slowly add eggs and egg substitute; beat until well blended. Beat in cornstarch, flour and vanilla. Beat in sour cream just until blended. Pour filling into prepared crust; place pan on baking sheet.

4. Bake 1 hour and 30 minutes to 1 hour and 40 minutes or until top of cheesecake is golden and just set. Cool completely in pan on wire rack. Refrigerate 8 hours or overnight. Garnish with strawberries, mint and graham cracker pieces.

Makes 18 servings

Nutrients per Serving: Calories: 154, Calories from Fat: 41%, Total Fat: 7g, Saturated Fat: 3g, Cholesterol: 47mg, Sodium: 296mg, Carbohydrate: 15g, Fiber: <1g, Protein: 10g

• Cakes & **Cheesecakes** •

Flourless Chocolate Cake

3 squares (1 ounce each) semisweet chocolate, chopped
3 tablespoons margarine
1 tablespoon espresso powder or instant coffee granules
2 tablespoons hot water
4 eggs, separated
2 egg whites
$^2/_3$ cup sugar, divided
3 tablespoons unsweetened cocoa powder, sifted
1 teaspoon vanilla
$^1/_2$ teaspoon salt
   Thawed fat-free whipped topping (optional)
   Fresh raspberries (optional)
   Fresh mint leaves (optional)

1. Preheat oven to 300°F. Grease 9-inch springform pan; line bottom of pan with parchment paper.

2. Melt chocolate and margarine in small heavy saucepan over low heat, stirring frequently; cool. Dissolve espresso powder in hot water in small bowl.

3. Place 6 egg whites in large bowl; set aside. Beat egg yolks in medium bowl with electric mixer at high speed about 5 minutes or until pale yellow in color. Add $^1/_3$ cup sugar; beat about 4 minutes or until mixture falls in ribbons from beaters. Slowly beat in melted chocolate mixture and espresso mixture at low speed just until blended. Beat in cocoa and vanilla just until blended.

4. Add salt to egg whites; beat at high speed 2 minutes or until soft peaks form. Beat in remaining $^1/_3$ cup sugar until stiff peaks form. Stir large spoonful of egg whites into chocolate mixture. Fold chocolate mixture into egg whites until almost blended. Spoon batter into prepared pan.

5. Bake 1 hour or until cake begins to pull away from side of pan. Cool on wire rack 10 minutes; run thin spatula around edge of cake. Carefully remove side of pan. Cool completely. Invert cake; remove bottom of pan and paper from cake. Cover and refrigerate at least 4 hours. Serve chilled with whipped topping, raspberries and mint, if desired.

Makes 10 servings

Nutrients per Serving: Calories: 190, Calories from Fat: 38%, Total Fat: 8g, Saturated Fat: 3g, Cholesterol: 85mg, Sodium: 240mg, Carbohydrate: 26g, Fiber: 1g, Protein: 4g

• Cakes & **Cheesecakes** •

Peanut Crumb Cake

1 package (about 18 ounces) yellow cake mix
³/₄ cup reduced-fat peanut butter
¹/₄ cup sucralose-brown sugar blend
1 cup water
³/₄ cup cholesterol-free egg substitute
¹/₄ cup vegetable oil
¹/₃ cup mini semisweet chocolate chips
¹/₄ cup peanut butter chips
¹/₄ cup roasted peanuts, finely chopped

1. Preheat oven to 350°F. Spray 13×9-inch baking pan with nonstick cooking spray.

2. Beat cake mix, peanut butter and sucralose-brown sugar blend in large bowl with electric mixer at low speed until mixture resembles coarse crumbs. Remove ¹/₃ cup to medium bowl for topping. Add water, egg substitute and oil to remaining mixture; beat at medium speed until well blended.

3. Spread batter evenly in prepared pan. Add chocolate chips, peanut butter chips and peanuts to reserved crumb mixture; mix well. Sprinkle over batter.

4. Bake 38 to 42 minutes or until toothpick inserted into center comes out clean. Cool cake completely in pan on wire rack.   *Makes 24 servings*

Nutrients per Serving: Calories: 203, Calories from Fat: 44%, Total Fat: 10g, Saturated Fat: 2g, Cholesterol: 0mg, Sodium: 226mg, Carbohydrate: 25g, Fiber: 1g, Protein: 4g

Peanut Crumb Cake

Shortcakes with Berries and Creamy Lemon Sauce

Berries

$^1\!/_2$ **(16-ounce) package frozen unsweetened mixed berries, thawed, including any juices**

1 **tablespoon sugar substitute**

$^1\!/_2$ **teaspoon vanilla**

Sauce

$^1\!/_2$ **(8-ounce) container thawed sugar-free whipped topping**

2 **tablespoons sugar substitute**

2 **tablespoons lemon juice**

2 **tablespoons fat-free (skim) milk**

Shortcake

1$^1\!/_2$ **cups biscuit baking mix**

$^1\!/_3$ **cup fat-free (skim) milk**

2 **tablespoons sugar substitute**

$^1\!/_2$ **teaspoon grated lemon peel**

Fresh mint leaves (optional)

1. Preheat oven to 425°F. Spray nonstick baking sheet with nonstick cooking spray.

2. Combine berries, 1 tablespoon sugar substitute and vanilla in medium bowl; set aside. Combine whipped topping, 2 tablespoons sugar substitute, lemon juice and 2 tablespoons milk in separate medium bowl; mix well. Refrigerate until ready to serve.

3. Combine baking mix, $^1\!/_3$ cup milk, 2 tablespoons sugar substitute and lemon peel in large bowl. Stir just until blended. Spoon batter onto prepared baking sheet in six equal mounds.

4. Bake 10 minutes or until golden. Cool on wire rack. Cut shortcakes in half horizontally. Top each bottom half with berries, sauce and top half of shortcake. Garnish with mint. *Makes 6 servings*

Nutrients per Serving (1 shortcake, $^1\!/_3$ cup berries and 2 tablespoons sauce): Calories: 191, Calories from Fat: 29%, Total Fat: 7g, Saturated Fat: 3g, Cholesterol: <1mg, Sodium: 380mg, Carbohydrate: 33g, Fiber: 1g, Protein: 3g

•Cakes & **Cheesecakes**•

Chilled Cherry Cheesecake

4 whole chocolate graham crackers, crushed (1 cup crumbs)
1 envelope (¹/₄ ounce) unflavored gelatin
¹/₄ cup cold water
12 ounces reduced-fat cream cheese, softened
6 ounces vanilla fat-free yogurt
¹/₄ cup sugar
1 teaspoon vanilla
1 can (20 ounces) light cherry pie filling

1. Press cracker crumbs onto bottom of 8-inch square baking pan. Sprinkle gelatin over water in small microwavable bowl; let stand 2 minutes. Microwave on HIGH 40 seconds; stir. Let stand 2 minutes or until gelatin is completely dissolved.

2. Beat cream cheese, yogurt, sugar and vanilla in medium bowl with electric mixer at medium speed until smooth.

3. Gradually beat gelatin mixture into cream cheese mixture at low speed until well blended. Pour into prepared crust; refrigerate until firm. Spoon cherry filling onto cheesecake. Refrigerate until ready to serve. *Makes 9 servings*

Nutrients per Serving: Calories: 221, Calories from Fat: 39%, Total Fat: 10g, Saturated Fat: 6g, Cholesterol: 29mg, Sodium: 226mg, Carbohydrate: 29g, Fiber: 1g, Protein: 5g

Tip Reduced-fat cream cheese is also known as Neufchâtel. It contains less fat and calories than regular cream cheese and can be used successfully in most recipes that call for regular cream cheese.

• Cakes & Cheesecakes •

Apple Walnut Cake

2¹⁄₂ cups chopped sliced Granny Smith apples (about 2 large apples)

³⁄₄ cup all-purpose flour

2 teaspoons baking powder

1¹⁄₂ teaspoons apple pie spice

³⁄₄ teaspoon salt

³⁄₄ cup sugar substitute*

¹⁄₄ cup plus 2 tablespoons packed brown sugar

4¹⁄₂ tablespoons margarine or butter, melted

³⁄₄ cup fat-free (skim) milk

3 eggs

1¹⁄₂ teaspoons vanilla

¹⁄₂ cup chopped walnuts

This recipe was tested with sucralose-based sugar substitute.

1. Preheat oven to 350°F. Spray 8 -or 9-inch square baking pan with nonstick cooking spray. Place apples in prepared pan.

2. Combine flour, baking powder, apple pie spice and salt in small bowl.

3. Whisk sugar substitute, brown sugar and margarine in medium bowl until blended. Whisk in milk, eggs and vanilla. Stir in flour mixture until smooth. Pour over apples. Sprinkle walnuts over batter.

4. Bake 45 to 55 minutes or until knife inserted into center comes out clean and apples are tender. Cool 10 minutes. Serve warm; refrigerate leftovers.

Makes 9 servings

Nutrients per Serving: Calories: 204, Calories from Fat: 53%, Total Fat: 12g, Saturated Fat: 2g, Cholesterol: 71mg, Sodium: 403mg, Carbohydrate: 23g, Fiber: 2g, Protein: 5g

Chocolate-Strawberry Layer Cake

$1^1/_2$ cups all-purpose flour
$^3/_4$ cup sucralose-sugar blend
1 teaspoon baking powder
1 teaspoon baking soda
$^1/_4$ teaspoon salt
1 cup water
$^1/_3$ cup unsweetened cocoa powder
2 tablespoons butter
$^1/_2$ teaspoon instant espresso powder or instant coffee powder (optional)
$^1/_3$ cup low-fat buttermilk
$^1/_3$ cup cholesterol-free egg substitute
3 tablespoons canola oil
2 teaspoons vanilla
$^1/_3$ cup sugar-free strawberry preserves
$^3/_4$ cup thawed fat-free whipped topping, plus additional for garnish
Fresh strawberry slices and fresh mint leaves (optional)

1. Preheat oven to 350°F. Spray two 8-inch round baking pans with nonstick cooking spray. Line bottoms of pans with parchment paper or waxed paper.

2. Combine flour, sucralose-sugar blend, baking powder, baking soda and salt in large bowl. Combine water, cocoa, butter and espresso powder, if desired, in small saucepan. Cook over medium heat, stirring constantly, until butter melts. Let stand 5 minutes.

3. Gradually add cocoa mixture to flour mixture with electric mixer at low speed, beating just until combined. *Do not overbeat.* Add buttermilk, egg substitute, oil and vanilla; beat at medium speed 1 minute or until smooth. Pour into prepared pans.

4. Bake about 20 minutes or until toothpick inserted into centers comes out clean. Cool in pans on wire racks 5 minutes. Invert onto wire racks; cool completely.

5. Place one cake layer, bottom side up, on cake plate. Spread strawberry preserves over cake. Top with $^3/_4$ cup whipped topping and remaining cake layer, bottom side down. Garnish with additional whipped topping, strawberry slices and mint.

Makes 16 servings

Nutrients per Serving: Calories: 162, Calories from Fat: 22%, Total Fat: 4g, Saturated Fat: 1g, Cholesterol: 4mg, Sodium: 179mg, Carbohydrate: 26g, Fiber: 1g, Protein: 1g

• Cakes & **Cheesecakes** •

Spicy Pumpkin Pie Cake

1³/₄ cups all-purpose flour
³/₄ cup sucralose-brown sugar blend
2 teaspoons ground cinnamon
1³/₄ teaspoons baking powder
1 teaspoon baking soda
¹/₂ teaspoon ground ginger
¹/₄ teaspoon salt
¹/₄ teaspoon ground cloves
1 can (15 ounces) solid-pack pumpkin
1 cup cholesterol-free egg substitute
²/₃ cup vegetable oil
1 cup raisins
Powdered sugar (optional)

1. Preheat oven to 350°F. Spray 13×9-inch baking pan with nonstick cooking spray.

2. Combine flour, sucralose-brown sugar blend, cinnamon, baking powder, baking soda, ginger, salt and cloves in large bowl. Add pumpkin, egg substitute and oil; beat with electric mixer at medium speed 2 minutes or until well blended. Stir in raisins. Pour into prepared pan.

3. Bake about 30 minutes or until toothpick inserted into center comes out clean. Cool completely in pan on wire rack. Just before serving, lightly sift powdered sugar over cake, if desired. *Makes 16 servings*

Nutrients per Serving: Calories: 221, Calories from Fat: 37%, Total Fat: 9g, Saturated Fat: 1g, Cholesterol: 0mg, Sodium: 200mg, Carbohydrate: 30g, Fiber: 2g, Protein: 4g

• Cakes & Cheesecakes •

Hot Skillet Pineapple Orange Snack Cake

- 1 can (8 ounces) crushed pineapple in juice, undrained
- 1 cup orange juice, divided
- 2 tablespoons packed dark brown sugar
- 1⅓ cups all-purpose flour
- ¼ cup granulated sugar
- ¼ cup powdered nonfat milk
- 2 teaspoons baking powder
- ½ teaspoon grated orange peel
- 3 egg whites
- 2 tablespoons canola oil
- 1 teaspoon vanilla

1. Preheat oven to 350°F.

2. Drain pineapple; reserve liquid. Combine pineapple juice and ½ cup orange juice in 10-inch ovenproof skillet; bring to a boil over high heat. Boil 2 to 3 minutes or until liquid measures ¼ cup. Remove from heat; stir in brown sugar until blended. Spoon pineapple evenly over brown sugar mixture. *Do not stir.*

3. Combine flour, granulated sugar, powdered milk, baking powder and orange peel in medium bowl. Add remaining ½ cup orange juice, egg whites, oil and vanilla; beat with electric mixer at low speed until blended. Beat at medium speed 2 minutes or until smooth. Spoon batter evenly over pineapple.

4. Bake 30 to 35 minutes or until toothpick inserted into center comes out clean. Cool on wire rack 5 minutes. Loosen edge of cake with knife and place serving plate over skillet. Invert cake onto plate, scraping any remaining pineapple from skillet and spooning on top of cake. Cut into wedges and serve warm.   *Makes 8 servings*

Nutrients per Serving: Calories: 187, Calories from Fat: 18%, Total Fat: 4g, Saturated Fat: <1g, Cholesterol: <1mg, Sodium: 165mg, Carbohydrate: 33g, Fiber: <1g, Protein: 5g

Hot Skillet Pineapple Orange Snack Cake

·Chocolate· Bliss

Chewy Mocha Brownie Cookies

1 cup all-purpose flour
$^1/_4$ teaspoon baking soda
$^1/_4$ cup stick margarine
$^2/_3$ cup granulated sugar
$^1/_3$ cup unsweetened cocoa powder
$^1/_4$ cup packed brown sugar
1$^1/_2$ teaspoons instant coffee granules
$^1/_4$ cup reduced-fat buttermilk
1 teaspoon vanilla
2 tablespoons powdered sugar

1. Combine flour and baking soda in small bowl. Melt margarine in medium saucepan; remove from heat. Stir in granulated sugar, cocoa, brown sugar and coffee granules. Add buttermilk and vanilla; mix well. Stir in flour mixture just until combined. Transfer dough to medium bowl. Cover and refrigerate 1 hour. (Dough will be stiff.)

2. Preheat oven to 350°F. Spray cookie sheets with nonstick cooking spray or line with parchment paper. Drop dough by rounded teaspoonfuls onto prepared cookie sheets.

3. Bake 10 to 11 minutes or until edges are firm. Cool cookies on cookie sheets 2 minutes. Remove to wire racks; cool completely.

4. Sprinkle with powdered sugar just before serving.   *Makes 24 cookies*

Nutrients per Serving (2 cookies): Calories: 142, Calories from Fat: 25%, Total Fat: 4g, Saturated Fat: 1g, Cholesterol: 0mg, Sodium: 69mg, Carbohydrate: 26g, Fiber: 1g, Protein: 2g

• Chocolate **Bliss** •

Chocolate Mousse Minis

    1 envelope (¹/₄ ounce) unflavored gelatin
¹/₄ cup water
³/₄ cup reduced-fat evaporated milk
¹/₃ cup unsweetened cocoa powder
    1 egg yolk
¹/₂ cup sugar substitute*
¹/₃ cup semisweet chocolate chips
¹/₂ teaspoon vanilla
³/₄ cup plus 6 tablespoons thawed reduced-fat whipped topping, divided
    3 chocolate wafer cookies, crumbled

This recipe was tested with sucralose-based sugar substitute.

1. Sprinkle gelatin over water in medium saucepan. Let stand about 2 minutes or until gelatin softens. Whisk in evaporated milk, cocoa and egg yolk. Cook and stir over low heat 2 minutes or until mixture is smooth and slightly thickened. Remove from heat.

2. Whisk in sugar substitute, chocolate chips and vanilla until smooth. Transfer to medium bowl; cool to room temperature, stirring every 5 minutes.

3. Fold in ³/₄ cup whipped topping. Spoon about ¹/₄ cup mousse into each of six 4-ounce dessert glasses. Cover and refrigerate 1 hour.

4. To serve, top each glass with 1 tablespoon whipped topping and 1¹/₂ teaspoons cookie crumbs. *Makes 6 servings*

Nutrients per Serving: Calories: 138, Calories from Fat: 46%, Total Fat: 7g, Saturated Fat: 3g, Cholesterol: 40mg, Sodium: 58mg, Carbohydrate: 19g, Fiber: 2g, Protein: 5g

• Chocolate **Bliss** •

Chocolate Spice Bundt Cake with Orange Glaze

1 package (about 18 ounces) devil's food cake mix
1¹/₃ cups water
³/₄ cup cholesterol-free egg substitute
2 tablespoons canola oil
1 tablespoon instant coffee granules
1 tablespoon grated orange peel
1 teaspoon ground cinnamon
¹/₂ cup orange juice
1 teaspoon cornstarch

1. Preheat oven to 325°F. Spray 12-cup bundt pan with nonstick cooking spray.

2. Beat cake mix, water, egg substitute, oil, coffee granules, orange peel and cinnamon in large bowl with electric mixer at medium speed until well blended. Pour batter into prepared pan.

3. Bake 35 to 37 minutes or until toothpick inserted near center comes out clean. Cool in pan on wire rack 10 minutes. Invert onto wire rack; cool completely.

4. Combine orange juice and cornstarch in small saucepan; stir until cornstarch is dissolved. Bring to a boil over medium-high heat. Boil 1 minute or until thickened. Cool completely. Spoon over cake.   *Makes 16 servings*

Variations: For deeper coffee flavor, add additional 1 tablespoon coffee granules to cake batter. For deeper chocolate flavor, add 1 tablespoon unsweetened cocoa powder to cake batter.

Nutrients per Serving: Calories: 164, Calories from Fat: 35%, Total Fat: 7g, Saturated Fat: 1g, Cholesterol: 0mg, Sodium: 289mg, Carbohydrate: 25g, Fiber: 1g, Protein: 3g

Chocolate Spice Bundt Cake with Orange Glaze

• Chocolate **Bliss** •

Old-Fashioned Chocolate Cream Pie

1 (9-inch) frozen pie crust
³⁄₄ cup sugar substitute*
¹⁄₂ cup unsweetened cocoa powder
¹⁄₄ cup cornstarch
¹⁄₄ teaspoon salt
3 cups fat-free (skim) milk, divided
¹⁄₄ cup cholesterol-free egg substitute
2 teaspoons vanilla
1 cup thawed fat-free whipped topping

This recipe was tested with sucralose-based sugar substitute.

1. Bake pie crust according to package directions for prebaked crust. Cool on wire rack.

2. Combine sugar substitute, cocoa, cornstarch and salt in medium saucepan. Slowly stir in 1 cup milk and egg substitute; let stand 5 minutes. Meanwhile, microwave remaining 2 cups milk on HIGH 2¹⁄₂ to 3 minutes or until hot but not boiling.

3. Slowly whisk hot milk into cocoa mixture in saucepan. Cook over medium heat, stirring frequently, 4 to 6 minutes or until mixture comes to a boil. Boil 30 seconds, stirring constantly. Remove from heat; place plastic wrap on surface of pudding. Cool to room temperature.

4. Spread filling in prepared crust. Cover and refrigerate at least 2 hours. Spread whipped topping over filling just before serving. *Makes 7 servings*

Nutrients per Serving: Calories: 184, Calories from Fat: 34%, Total Fat: 7g, Saturated Fat: 1g, Cholesterol: 2mg, Sodium: 268mg, Carbohydrate: 28g, Fiber: 2g, Protein: 6g

• Chocolate **Bliss** •

Chocolate Chip, Banana and Marshmallow Triangles

1 package (6¹/₂ ounces) chocolate chip muffin mix
¹/₂ cup water
1 medium banana, sliced
¹/₂ cup mini marshmallows
¹/₃ cup coarsely chopped pecans

1. Preheat oven to 375°F. Spray nonstick 8-inch square baking pan with nonstick cooking spray.

2. Combine muffin mix and water in medium bowl just until blended. Spoon into prepared pan. Layer banana slices over batter; sprinkle with marshmallows and pecans.

3. Bake 30 minutes or until marshmallows begin to brown. Cool completely on wire rack. Cut into 4 squares; cut each square in half diagonally to create 8 triangles.

Makes 8 servings

Tip: For more flavor, toast the pecans before using. Cook pecans in a small skillet over medium heat 3 to 5 minutes or until lightly browned, stirring constantly. Transfer to a plate to cool.

Nutrients per Serving: Calories: 151, Calories from Fat: 35%, Total Fat: 6g, Saturated Fat: 1g, Cholesterol: 1mg, Sodium: 106mg, Carbohydrate: 24g, Fiber: 1g, Protein: 2g

Tip When buying bananas, look for plump, evenly-colored yellow skins. Bananas with green tips and ridges will ripen at home within a day or two. To speed ripening, place the bananas in an unsealed paper bag at room temperature.

• Chocolate **Bliss** •

Chocolate Orange Bread Pudding

¼ cup sugar

3 tablespoons unsweetened cocoa powder

1½ cups fat-free (skim) milk

3 eggs, lightly beaten

1 to 2 teaspoons grated orange peel

1 teaspoon vanilla

¾ teaspoon ground cinnamon

4 ounces (4 cups) cubed French baguette

¼ cup sugar-free chocolate ice cream topping

8 maraschino cherries with stems (optional)

1. Preheat oven to 350°F. Combine sugar and cocoa in medium bowl; stir in milk, eggs, orange peel, vanilla and cinnamon.

2. Place bread cubes in ungreased 8-inch square baking dish. Pour milk mixture over bread cubes.

3. Bake about 35 minutes or until knife inserted near center comes out clean. Cool 5 to 10 minutes.

4. Spoon warm pudding into dessert dishes. Drizzle with ice cream topping and garnish with a cherry.   *Makes 8 servings*

Nutrients per Serving: Calories: 131, Calories from Fat: 14%, Total Fat: 2g, Saturated Fat: <1g, Cholesterol: 80mg, Sodium: 131mg, Carbohydrate: 23g, Fiber: 1g, Protein: 6g

Chocolate Orange Bread Pudding

• Chocolate **Bliss** •

Chocolate Cookie Parfaits

1 package (4-serving size) chocolate fat-free sugar-free instant pudding and pie filling mix
2 cups fat-free (skim) milk
8 tablespoons thawed reduced-fat whipped topping
4 sugar-free chocolate sandwich cookies, finely crushed
4 teaspoons multi-colored sprinkles

1. Prepare pudding according to package directions using 2 cups milk.

2. Spoon half of pudding into four parfait glasses. Spread 1 tablespoon whipped topping over pudding in each glass. Sprinkle with half of crushed cookies. Spoon remaining pudding over cookies. Top with remaining whipped topping, cookies and sprinkles. *Makes 4 servings*

Nutrients per Serving: Calories: 158, Calories from Fat: 34%, Total Fat: 6g, Saturated Fat: 2g, Cholesterol: 2mg, Sodium: 387mg, Carbohydrate: 24g, Fiber: 0g, Protein: 6g

Chocolate Cinnamon Cake

1 package (about 18 ounces) devil's food cake mix
1¼ cups water
¾ cup cholesterol-free egg substitute *or* 3 eggs
⅓ cup canola oil
1 tablespoon instant coffee granules
1½ to 2 teaspoons ground cinnamon
¼ cup powdered sugar

1. Preheat oven to 350°F. Spray 13×9-inch baking pan with nonstick cooking spray.

2. Combine cake mix, water, egg substitute, oil, coffee granules and cinnamon in large bowl; mix according to package directions. Pour batter into prepared pan.

3. Bake 25 to 27 minutes or until toothpick inserted into center comes out clean. Cool completely on wire rack.

4. Just before serving, sift powdered sugar over cake. *Makes 18 to 20 servings*

Nutrients per Serving: Calories: 170, Calories from Fat: 43%, Total Fat: 9g, Saturated Fat: 1g, Cholesterol: 0mg, Sodium: 256mg, Carbohydrate: 22g, Fiber: <1g, Protein: 2g

• Chocolate **Bliss** •

Devil's Food Ice Cream Cake with Java Cream

1 package (about 18 ounces) reduced-sugar devil's food cake mix
1¼ cups plus 2 tablespoons water, divided
¾ cup cholesterol-free egg substitute
2 tablespoons canola oil
1½ tablespoons instant coffee granules
12 ounces thawed fat-free whipped topping
3 cups vanilla fat-free ice cream, softened

1. Preheat oven to 350°F. Spray two 9-inch round baking pans with nonstick cooking spray.

2. Beat cake mix, 1¼ cups water, egg substitute and oil in large bowl with electric mixer at medium speed 2 minutes. Pour batter into prepared pans.

3. Bake 20 to 25 minutes or until toothpick inserted into centers comes out almost clean. Cool in pans on wire racks 10 minutes. Invert onto wire racks; cool completely.

4. Combine remaining 2 tablespoons water and coffee granules in medium bowl; stir until coffee is dissolved. Fold in whipped topping.

5. Place one cake layer on cake plate; spread evenly with ice cream and top with remaining cake layer. Frost side and top of cake with whipped topping mixture. Freeze until ready to serve. Store leftovers in freezer. *Makes 18 servings*

Note: Bake 30 to 35 minutes if using 8-inch round baking pans.

Nutrients per Serving: Calories: 195, Calories from Fat: 19%, Total Fat: 4g, Saturated Fat: <1g, Cholesterol: 0mg, Sodium: 126mg, Carbohydrate: 36g, Fiber: <1g, Protein: 3g

• Chocolate **Bliss** •

Rocky Road Pudding

5 tablespoons unsweetened cocoa powder
$\frac{1}{4}$ cup granulated sugar
3 tablespoons cornstarch
$\frac{1}{8}$ teaspoon salt
2$\frac{1}{2}$ cups low-fat (1%) milk
2 egg yolks, beaten
2 teaspoons vanilla
6 packets sugar substitute *or* equivalent of $\frac{1}{4}$ cup sugar
1 cup mini marshmallows
$\frac{1}{4}$ cup chopped walnuts, toasted

1. Combine cocoa, granulated sugar, cornstarch and salt in small saucepan; mix well. Stir in milk until smooth. Cook over medium-high heat, stirring constantly, about 10 minutes or until mixture thickens and begins to boil.

2. Add $\frac{1}{2}$ cup milk mixture to egg yolks in small bowl; beat well. Pour mixture back into saucepan. Cook over medium heat 10 minutes or until mixture reaches 160°F. Remove from heat; stir in vanilla.

3. Place plastic wrap on surface of pudding. Refrigerate about 20 minutes or until slightly cooled. Stir in sugar substitute. Spoon pudding into six dessert dishes; top with marshmallows and walnuts.   *Makes 6 servings*

Nutrients per Serving: Calories: 190, Calories from Fat: 28%, Total Fat: 6g, Saturated Fat: 1g, Cholesterol: 75mg, Sodium: 121mg, Carbohydrate: 28g, Fiber: <1g, Protein: 7g

Rocky Road Pudding

• Chocolate **Bliss** •

Rocky Road Pudding

5 tablespoons unsweetened cocoa powder
$\frac{1}{4}$ cup granulated sugar
3 tablespoons cornstarch
$\frac{1}{8}$ teaspoon salt
$2\frac{1}{2}$ cups low-fat (1%) milk
2 egg yolks, beaten
2 teaspoons vanilla
6 packets sugar substitute *or* equivalent of $\frac{1}{4}$ cup sugar
1 cup mini marshmallows
$\frac{1}{4}$ cup chopped walnuts, toasted

1. Combine cocoa, granulated sugar, cornstarch and salt in small saucepan; mix well. Stir in milk until smooth. Cook over medium-high heat, stirring constantly, about 10 minutes or until mixture thickens and begins to boil.

2. Add $\frac{1}{2}$ cup milk mixture to egg yolks in small bowl; beat well. Pour mixture back into saucepan. Cook over medium heat 10 minutes or until mixture reaches 160°F. Remove from heat; stir in vanilla.

3. Place plastic wrap on surface of pudding. Refrigerate about 20 minutes or until slightly cooled. Stir in sugar substitute. Spoon pudding into six dessert dishes; top with marshmallows and walnuts. *Makes 6 servings*

Nutrients per Serving: Calories: 190, Calories from Fat: 28%, Total Fat: 6g, Saturated Fat: 1g, Cholesterol: 75mg, Sodium: 121mg, Carbohydrate: 28g, Fiber: <1g, Protein: 7g

• Chocolate **Bliss** •

Chocolate Pudding Cake Squares

1 cup all-purpose flour
$1/2$ cup warm fat-free (skim) milk
$1/3$ cup plus $1/4$ cup granulated sugar, divided
20 packets sugar substitute *or* equivalent of 40 teaspoons sugar, divided
6 tablespoons unsweetened cocoa powder, divided
2 tablespoons canola oil
2 teaspoons baking powder
2 teaspoons vanilla
$1/2$ teaspoon salt
$1^3/4$ cups boiling water

1. Preheat oven to 350°F. Beat flour, milk, $1/3$ cup granulated sugar, 10 packets sugar substitute, 3 tablespoons cocoa, oil, baking powder, vanilla and salt in large bowl with electric mixer at medium speed 2 minutes or until well blended. Pour into ungreased 9-inch square baking pan.

2. Sprinkle remaining $1/4$ cup granulated sugar, 10 packets sugar substitute and 3 tablespoons cocoa over batter in pan. Pour boiling water over top. *Do not stir.*

3. Bake 40 minutes or until cake has risen to top of pan and sauce is bubbly around edges. Cool 10 minutes; cut into squares. Serve warm. *Makes 9 servings*

Nutrients per Serving: Calories: 150, Calories from Fat: 18%, Total Fat: 3g, Saturated Fat: <1g, Cholesterol: <1mg, Sodium: 246mg, Carbohydrate: 26g, Fiber: <1g, Protein: 4g

171 calories

·Classic·
Sweets

Mango-Raspberry Crisp

1 mango, peeled, seeded and chopped into $1/2$-inch pieces
1 cup fresh raspberries
$1/2$ cup old-fashioned oats
2 tablespoons packed brown sugar
$1/2$ to 1 teaspoon ground cinnamon
4 teaspoons butter
2 tablespoons chopped pecans

1. Preheat oven to 400°F. Spray four 6-ounce custard cups or ramekins with nonstick cooking spray.

2. Divide mango and raspberries evenly among custard cups.

3. Combine oats, brown sugar and cinnamon in medium bowl. Cut in butter with pastry blender or two knives until mixture resembles coarse crumbs. Stir in pecans. Sprinkle evenly over fruit.

4. Bake 20 to 25 minutes or until fruit is tender and topping is golden brown. Let stand 15 minutes before serving. *Makes 4 servings*

Nutrients per Serving: Calories: 171, Calories from Fat: 37%, Total Fat: 7g, Saturated Fat: 3g, Cholesterol: 10mg, Sodium: 31mg, Carbohydrate: 27g, Fiber: 4g, Protein: 2g

Glazed Plum Pastry

3 tablespoons sucralose-sugar blend, divided
2 tablespoons all-purpose flour
1 package (about 17 ounces) frozen puff pastry sheets, thawed
8 plums (about 2 pounds)
$1/4$ teaspoon ground cinnamon
$1/3$ cup sugar-free apricot preserves

1. Preheat oven to 400°F. Line 18×12-inch baking sheet with parchment paper. Combine 2 tablespoons sucralose-sugar blend and flour in small bowl.

2. Unfold pastry sheets on prepared baking sheet. Place pastry sheets side by side so fold lines are parallel to length of baking sheet. Arrange sheets so they overlap $1/2$ inch in center. Press center seam firmly to seal. Trim ends so pastry fits on baking sheet. Prick entire surface of pastry with fork.

3. Sprinkle sugar blend-flour mixture evenly over pastry to within $1/2$ inch of edges. Bake 12 to 15 minutes or until pastry is slightly puffed and golden.

4. Cut plums in half lengthwise; remove pits. Cut crosswise into $1/8$-inch-thick slices. Arrange slices slightly overlapping in five rows down length of pastry. Combine remaining 1 tablespoon sucralose-sugar blend and cinnamon in small bowl; sprinkle evenly over plums.

5. Bake 15 minutes or until plums are tender and pastry is browned. Remove to wire rack.

6. Microwave preserves in small microwavable bowl on HIGH 30 to 40 seconds or until melted. Brush preserves over plums. Cool 10 to 15 minutes before serving.

Makes 20 servings

Nutrients per Serving: Calories: 152, Calories from Fat: 47%, Total Fat: 8g, Saturated Fat: 2g, Cholesterol: 0mg, Sodium: 53mg, Carbohydrate: 18g, Fiber: 1g, Protein: 2g

148 calories

Individual Tiramisù Cups

4 whole ladyfingers, broken into bite-size pieces
6 tablespoons cold strong coffee *or* ½ teaspoon instant coffee granules dissolved in ⅓ cup water
2 packets sugar substitute
½ teaspoon vanilla
½ cup thawed fat-free whipped topping
1½ teaspoons unsweetened cocoa powder
1 tablespoon sliced almonds

1. Divide ladyfinger pieces between two 6-ounce custard cups.

2. Combine coffee, sugar substitute and vanilla in small bowl; stir until sugar substitute is dissolved. Spoon half of coffee mixture over each serving.

3. Place whipped topping in small bowl; fold in cocoa. Spoon mixture over ladyfingers. Cover and refrigerate at least 2 hours.

4. Meanwhile, toast almonds in small skillet over medium-high heat 2 to 3 minutes or until golden brown, stirring constantly. Transfer to small bowl; cool completely.

5. Sprinkle almonds over desserts just before serving. *Makes 2 servings*

Nutrients per Serving: Calories: 148, Calories from Fat: 28%, Total Fat: 5g, Saturated Fat: 1g, Cholesterol: 80mg, Sodium: 43mg, Carbohydrate: 22g, Fiber: 1g, Protein: 4g

Tip Tiramisù is a traditional Italian dessert whose name means "pick me up." It can be considered a trifle since ingredients are layered. Although many variations exist, ladyfingers and coffee are two essential ingredients in any tiramisù recipe.

Individual Tiramisù Cup

● Classic **Sweets** ●

Fruit-Filled Cream Puffs

1 cup water
1/3 cup canola oil
2 tablespoons sugar
1/4 teaspoon salt
1 cup all-purpose flour
2 eggs
2 egg whites
1 3/4 cups fat-free (skim) milk
1 package (4-serving size) vanilla fat-free sugar-free instant pudding and pie filling mix
2 cups fresh berries, such as sliced strawberries, raspberries or blueberries

1. Preheat oven to 400°F. Spray large baking sheet with nonstick cooking spray or line with parchment paper.

2. Bring water, oil, sugar and salt to a boil in medium saucepan. Add flour all at once, stirring vigorously until dough pulls away from side of pan (about 1 minute). Immediately remove from heat; cool at least 5 minutes.

3. Add eggs and egg whites, one at a time, beating with spoon or whisk after each addition until completely incorporated. Drop dough by scant 1/4 cupfuls into 10 mounds about 3 inches apart onto prepared baking sheet.

4. Bake 30 to 35 minutes or until dry and golden brown. Remove to wire rack; cool completely. Meanwhile, whisk milk and pudding mix in medium bowl about 2 minutes or until thickened.

5. Cut off top third of each cream puff and remove any strands of soft dough. Fill bottoms with pudding and berries; replace tops. Serve immediately or cover and refrigerate until ready to serve. *Makes 10 servings*

Nutrients per Serving: Calories: 137, Calories from Fat: 53%, Total Fat: 8g, Saturated Fat: 1g, Cholesterol: 42mg, Sodium: 83mg, Carbohydrate: 12g, Fiber: <1g, Protein: 3g

Fruit-Filled Cream Puff

• Classic **Sweets** •

Upside-Down Apples

$^1/_4$ **cup finely chopped pecans or walnuts**
$^1/_4$ **cup chopped dried apricots or any dried fruit**
$^1/_2$ **teaspoon ground cinnamon**
$^1/_2$ **teaspoon vanilla**
$^1/_4$ **teaspoon ground nutmeg**
$^1/_8$ **teaspoon salt**
  2 **tablespoons honey or maple syrup**
  2 **Fuji apples (about 8 ounces each), halved and cored**
  1 **cup vanilla sugar-free ice cream**

1. Preheat oven to 350°F. Spray 9-inch pie pan with nonstick cooking spray.

2. Combine pecans, apricots, cinnamon, vanilla, nutmeg and salt in prepared pan; mix well. Spread evenly over bottom of pan. Drizzle with honey. Place apple halves in nut mixture, cut side down. Cover with foil.

3. Bake 35 minutes or just until tender. Spoon nut mixture over each apple half. Serve with ice cream. *Makes 4 servings*

Nutrients per Serving (1 apple half with 2 tablespoons nut mixture and $^1/_4$ cup ice cream): Calories: 187, Calories from Fat: 29%, Total Fat: 7g, Saturated Fat: 1g, Cholesterol: 5mg, Sodium: 109mg, Carbohydrate: 32g, Fiber: 4g, Protein: 4g

Tip Fuji apples are a combination of Red Delicious and Ralls Janet apples. They are crisp and juicy apples that hold their shape when baking. If Fuji apples are not available, substitute Braeburn or Gala apples.

Upside-Down Apple

• Classic **Sweets** •

Panna Cotta with Mango Sauce

1½ teaspoons unflavored gelatin
3 tablespoons cold water
¾ cup fat-free half-and-half
¼ cup plus 2 teaspoons sugar, divided
1 teaspoon grated lemon peel
¾ cup reduced-fat buttermilk
¾ cup fresh or frozen mango chunks
2 teaspoons lemon juice
Fresh mint leaves (optional)

1. Sprinkle gelatin over water in small heavy saucepan. Let stand about 2 minutes or until gelatin softens. Stir in half-and-half, ¼ cup sugar and lemon peel; cook and stir over low heat until gelatin is dissolved. *Do not boil*. Remove from heat; strain into medium bowl. Stir in buttermilk. Cool 20 minutes, stirring occasionally.

2. Divide mixture among four 6-ounce custard cups or ramekins. Cover and refrigerate at least 4 hours or until set.

3. Meanwhile, blend mango, lemon juice and remaining 2 teaspoons sugar in blender or food processor until smooth; strain into small bowl. Refrigerate until ready to serve.

4. Run thin knife around edge of each cup to loosen. Dip bottoms into bowl of warm water 5 seconds. Invert and unmold onto serving plates; serve with mango sauce. Garnish with mint. *Makes 4 servings*

Nutrients per Serving: Calories: 131, Calories from Fat: 3%, Total Fat: <1g, Saturated Fat: <1g, Cholesterol: 9mg, Sodium: 95mg, Carbohydrate: 27g, Fiber: 1g, Protein: 4g

Panna Cotta with Mango Sauce

• Classic **Sweets** •

Cherry Cobbler

1 sheet frozen puff pastry, thawed
2 teaspoons fat-free (skim) milk
$1/2$ cup plus 1 teaspoon sucralose-sugar blend, divided
$1/4$ teaspoon plus $1/8$ teaspoon ground cinnamon, divided
$1 1/2$ pounds frozen unsweetened tart or sweet cherries
3 tablespoons quick-cooking tapioca
1 teaspoon almond extract
2 tablespoons cold margarine, cut into small pieces
Thawed fat-free whipped topping (optional)

1. Preheat oven to 400°F. Line baking sheet with parchment paper.

2. Unfold pastry sheet on lightly floured surface. Cut out 10 shapes with $2 1/2$-inch scalloped cookie cutter; discard trimmings. Place cut-outs on prepared baking sheet; lightly brush with milk. Combine 1 teaspoon sucralose-sugar blend and $1/8$ teaspoon cinnamon in small bowl; sprinkle over cut-outs.

3. Bake 12 to 15 minutes or until golden brown. Remove to wire rack to cool completely.

4. Meanwhile, spray 2-quart baking dish with nonstick cooking spray. Combine cherries, remaining $1/2$ cup sucralose-sugar blend, tapioca, almond extract and remaining $1/4$ teaspoon cinnamon in large bowl; mix well. Let stand 15 minutes. Spoon cherry mixture into prepared baking dish; dot with margarine pieces.

5. Bake 40 to 45 minutes or until hot and bubbly. Cool 5 minutes. Spoon $1/3$ cup cherry mixture into small dessert dish; top with pastry cut-out. Top each serving with whipped topping, if desired. *Makes 10 servings*

Nutrients per Serving ($1/3$ cup cherry mixture with 1 pastry cut-out): Calories: 184, Calories from Fat: 34%, Total Fat: 7g, Saturated Fat: 2g, Cholesterol: 0mg, Sodium: 59mg, Carbohydrate: 26g, Fiber: 1g, Protein: 2g

• Classic **Sweets** •

Enlightened Pumpkin Pie

$1/4$ cup coarsely crushed cornflakes

$1/4$ cup plus 1 tablespoon packed brown sugar, divided

1 teaspoon ground cinnamon, divided

$1/4$ teaspoon plus $1/8$ teaspoon ground ginger, divided

$3/4$ cup evaporated fat-free milk

$3/4$ cup solid-pack pumpkin

2 tablespoons corn syrup

1 teaspoon cornstarch

$1/4$ teaspoon ground nutmeg

$1/3$ cup cholesterol-free egg substitute

1. Preheat oven to 350°F. For topping, combine cornflakes, 1 tablespoon brown sugar, $1/2$ teaspoon cinnamon and $1/8$ teaspoon ginger in small bowl; mix well. Set aside.

2. For filling, heat milk in small saucepan over medium heat. *Do not boil.* Combine pumpkin, remaining $1/4$ cup brown sugar, corn syrup, cornstarch, remaining $1/2$ teaspoon cinnamon, $1/4$ teaspoon ginger and nutmeg in large bowl.

3. Stir hot milk into pumpkin mixture. Add egg substitute; stir until smooth. Pour into four 6-ounce ovenproof custard cups or ramekins. Sprinkle evenly with topping. Place cups in baking pan; carefully add hot water to $3/4$-inch depth.

4. Bake 35 to 40 minutes or until knife inserted into centers comes out clean.

Makes 4 servings

Nutrients per Serving: Calories: 172, Calories from Fat: 2%, Total Fat: <1g, Saturated Fat: <1g, Cholesterol: 2mg, Sodium: 133mg, Carbohydrate: 37g, Fiber: 1g, Protein: 6g

• Classic **Sweets** •

Peach Pecan Upside-Down Pancake

2 tablespoons butter, melted
2 tablespoons packed light brown sugar
1 tablespoon maple syrup
¹/₂ (16-ounce) package frozen unsweetened peach slices, thawed
3 tablespoons pecan pieces
²/₃ cup biscuit baking mix
2 eggs
¹/₃ cup fat-free (skim) milk
¹/₂ teaspoon vanilla
    Additional maple syrup (optional)

1. Preheat oven to 400°F. Spray 9-inch pie pan with nonstick cooking spray.

2. Pour butter into prepared pan. Sprinkle with brown sugar and maple syrup. Arrange peach slices in single layer over syrup. Sprinkle with pecans.

3. Place baking mix in medium bowl. Whisk eggs, milk and vanilla in small bowl; stir into baking mix just until moistened. Pour batter over peaches.

4. Bake 15 to 18 minutes or until lightly browned and toothpick inserted into center comes out clean. Cool 1 minute. Run knife around edge of pan. Invert pancake onto serving plate; cut into wedges. Serve immediately with additional maple syrup, if desired. *Makes 6 servings*

Nutrients per Serving: Calories: 175, Calories from Fat: 36%, Total Fat: 9g, Saturated Fat: 4g, Cholesterol: 82mg, Sodium: 223mg, Carbohydrate: 20g, Fiber: <1g, Protein: 4g

• Classic **Sweets** •

Dessert Nachos

  3 (6- to 7-inch) flour tortillas
    Nonstick cooking spray
  1 tablespoon sugar
  $1/8$ teaspoon ground cinnamon
    Dash ground allspice
  1 container (6 ounces) vanilla fat-free sugar-free yogurt
  1 teaspoon grated orange peel
$1^1/2$ cups fresh strawberries, stemmed and cut into quarters
  $1/2$ cup fresh blueberries
  4 teaspoons mini semisweet chocolate chips

1. Preheat oven to 375°F.

2. Cut each tortilla into eight wedges. Place on ungreased baking sheet. Generously spray tortilla wedges with cooking spray. Combine sugar, cinnamon and allspice in small bowl. Sprinkle over tortilla wedges. Bake 7 to 9 minutes or until lightly browned; cool completely.

3. Meanwhile, combine yogurt and orange peel in small bowl.

4. Place six tortilla wedges on each of four small plates. Top with strawberries and blueberries. Drizzle with yogurt mixture; sprinkle with chocolate chips. Serve immediately. *Makes 4 servings*

Nutrients per Serving (6 tortilla wedges with $1/2$ cup berries, $1/4$ cup yogurt mixture and 1 teaspoon chocolate chips): Calories: 160, Calories from Fat: 19%, Total Fat: 3g, Saturated Fat: 1g, Cholesterol: 2mg, Sodium: 146mg, Carbohydrate: 28g, Fiber: 3g, Protein: 4g

• Classic **Sweets** •

Sweet Potato Phyllo Wraps

$^3/_4$ **cup mashed cooked sweet potato**
$^3/_4$ **teaspoon vanilla**
$^1/_2$ **teaspoon ground cinnamon**
4 **($16^1/_2 \times 12$-inch) sheets frozen phyllo dough, thawed**
Butter-flavored cooking spray
4 **tablespoons finely chopped pecans**
1 **tablespoon light maple syrup**
Fresh strawberries (optional)

1. Preheat oven to 375°F. Line baking sheet with parchment paper. Combine sweet potato, vanilla and cinnamon in small bowl; mix well.

2. Unroll phyllo dough, keeping sheets stacked. Cover with large sheet of waxed paper and damp kitchen towel. Remove one sheet at a time; place on work surface with short side facing you. Spray edges lightly with cooking spray.

3. Spread 3 tablespoons sweet potato mixture across short edge of phyllo dough. Sprinkle with 1 tablespoon chopped pecans. Roll up. Cut into thirds; place on prepared baking sheet. Repeat with remaining phyllo sheets, sweet potato mixture and pecans. Spray tops of wraps with cooking spray.

4. Bake 15 to 20 minutes or until golden brown. Drizzle with maple syrup. Garnish with strawberries. *Makes 4 servings*

Nutrients per Serving (3 wraps with $^3/_4$ teaspoon maple syrup): Calories: 165, Calories from Fat: 38%, Total Fat: 7g, Saturated Fat: 1g, Cholesterol: 0mg, Sodium: 120mg, Carbohydrate: 24g, Fiber: 3g, Protein: 3g

• Classic **Sweets** •

So-Easy Peach Pie

1 (9-inch) refrigerated pie crust ($1/2$ of 15-ounce package)
1 package (16 ounces) frozen unsweetened peaches, thawed, juice reserved
2 teaspoons cornstarch
$1/2$ cup golden raisins
4 tablespoons sugar, divided
1 teaspoon vanilla
$1/4$ teaspoon ground cinnamon (optional)

1. Preheat oven to 450°F. Spray nonstick baking sheet with nonstick cooking spray.

2. Unroll crust on prepared baking sheet; roll or flute edge, if desired. Pierce crust several times with fork. Bake 10 to 12 minutes or until golden.

3. Combine peach juice and cornstarch in large nonstick skillet; stir until cornstarch is dissolved. Add peaches and raisins; bring to a boil over high heat. Boil 2 minutes, stirring occasionally. Remove from heat; add 3 tablespoons sugar, vanilla and cinnamon, if desired.

4. Slide baked pie crust over peach mixture in skillet. Sprinkle with remaining 1 tablespoon sugar. *Makes 8 servings*

Variation: Substitute 1 teaspoon almond extract for the vanilla.

Nutrients per Serving: Calories: 201, Calories from Fat: 31%, Total Fat: 7g, Saturated Fat: 3g, Cholesterol: 3mg, Sodium: 111mg, Carbohydrate: 33g, Fiber: 1g, Protein: 1g

·Cool &·
Creamy

Dreamy Orange Pie

8 whole low-fat honey graham crackers, crushed (1½ cups)
2 tablespoons reduced-fat margarine, melted
1 pint vanilla sugar-free ice cream, softened
1 pint orange sherbet, softened
10 tablespoons thawed sugar-free whipped topping
10 mandarin orange slices

1. Preheat oven to 350°F. Spray 9-inch springform pan with nonstick cooking spray.

2. Combine cracker crumbs and margarine in medium bowl. Gently press crumb mixture onto bottom and ½ inch up side of prepared pan. Bake 8 to 10 minutes or until lightly browned; cool completely on wire rack.

3. Spread ice cream in cooled crust. Freeze 30 minutes or until firm to the touch. Spread orange sherbet over ice cream; freeze at least 1 hour or until firm.

4. To serve, run knife around edge of pan; remove side of pan. Top each slice with 1 tablespoon whipped topping and 1 orange slice. *Makes 10 servings*

Nutrients per Serving: Calories: 160, Calories from Fat: 23%, Total Fat: 4g, Saturated Fat: 2g, Cholesterol: 4mg, Sodium: 139mg, Carbohydrate: 28g, Fiber: 2g, Protein: 3g

• Cool & **Creamy** •

Frozen Chocolate-Covered Bananas

2 medium bananas
4 wooden craft sticks
$^1/_2$ cup low-fat granola cereal without raisins
$^1/_3$ cup hot fudge topping, at room temperature

1. Line baking sheet with waxed paper.

2. Peel bananas; cut in half crosswise. Insert wooden stick into center of cut end of each banana about 1$^1/_2$ inches into banana half. Place on prepared baking sheet; freeze at least 2 hours or until firm.

3. Place granola in large resealable food storage bag; crush slightly using rolling pin or meat mallet. Transfer granola to shallow plate. Place hot fudge topping in shallow dish.

4. Place one frozen banana in hot fudge topping; turn and spread topping evenly over banana with spatula. Place banana on plate with granola; turn to coat. Return to baking sheet. Repeat with remaining bananas.

5. Freeze at least 2 hours or until hot fudge topping is very firm. Let stand 5 minutes before serving.   *Makes 4 servings*

Nutrients per Serving: Calories: 191, Calories from Fat: 19%, Total Fat: 4g, Saturated Fat: 2g, Cholesterol: 3mg, Sodium: 132mg, Carbohydrate: 38g, Fiber: 3g, Protein: 3g

Mango Cream Bowls

2 cups thawed fat-free whipped topping, divided
3 ounces reduced-fat tub-style cream cheese, at room temperature
3 tablespoons sugar substitute
½ teaspoon vanilla
1 medium fresh mango, diced *or* 1 cup diced jarred mango
½ teaspoon grated orange peel
¼ cup orange juice

1. Combine 1 cup whipped topping, cream cheese, sugar substitute and vanilla in medium bowl until well blended. Spoon into four 6-ounce ramekins. Top with mango.

2. Combine remaining 1 cup whipped topping, orange peel and juice in small bowl. Spoon mixture over mango. Serve immediately or cover and refrigerate until ready to serve.

Makes 4 servings

Nutrients per Serving: Calories: 142, Calories from Fat: 20%, Total Fat: 3g, Saturated Fat: 2g, Cholesterol: 10mg, Sodium: 121mg, Carbohydrate: 25g, Fiber: 1g, Protein: 2g

Tip One medium orange yields 1 to 2 tablespoons grated orange peel and about ⅓ cup juice. Extra grated orange peel may be tightly wrapped in plastic wrap and frozen.

• Cool & Creamy •

Cherry Bottom Pie

12 whole low-fat graham crackers, crumbled
4 tablespoons margarine, melted
3 tablespoons sucralose-sugar blend, divided
1 can (20 ounces) light cherry pie filling, divided
1 envelope ($\frac{1}{4}$ ounce) unflavored gelatin
$\frac{1}{4}$ cup cold water
$\frac{3}{4}$ cup boiling water
1 package (8 ounces) reduced-fat cream cheese, softened
1 teaspoon vanilla
$\frac{1}{2}$ (8-ounce) container thawed fat-free whipped topping
Chocolate shavings (optional)

1. Preheat oven to 350°F. Combine cracker crumbs, margarine and 1 tablespoon sucralose-sugar blend in medium bowl. Press crumb mixture evenly onto bottom and up side of 9-inch deep-dish pie pan. Bake 8 to 10 minutes; cool completely on wire rack.

2. Spread two thirds of pie filling over cooled crust. Cover remaining filling and refrigerate until ready to serve.

3. Combine gelatin and cold water in small bowl; let stand 5 minutes to soften. Add boiling water; stir until gelatin is completely dissolved. Cool gelatin mixture 5 to 10 minutes.

4. Beat cream cheese, remaining 2 tablespoons sucralose-sugar blend and vanilla in large bowl with electric mixer at medium speed until smooth. Slowly add $\frac{3}{4}$ cup gelatin mixture *(discard remaining $\frac{1}{4}$ cup gelatin mixture)*. Beat at low speed until blended. Stir in whipped topping until smooth. Pour cream cheese mixture over cherry filling in pie crust. Cover and refrigerate at least 3 hours or until firm.

5. Top with remaining pie filling. Sprinkle with chocolate shavings, if desired. Cover and refrigerate any remaining pie.   *Makes 10 servings*

Nutrients per Serving: Calories: 192, Calories from Fat: 38%, Total Fat: 8g, Saturated Fat: 3g, Cholesterol: 16mg, Sodium: 217mg, Carbohydrate: 25g, Fiber: 1g, Protein: 3g

Cherry Bottom Pie

• Cool & Creamy •

Bananas Foster Sundae

1 medium banana
2 tablespoons packed brown sugar
2 teaspoons butter
1 tablespoon water
1 teaspoon rum extract
2 cups vanilla reduced-fat sugar-free ice cream
  Wafer cookie pieces (optional)

1. Peel and cut banana crosswise into ¼-inch slices.

2. Heat brown sugar and butter in medium nonstick skillet over medium-low heat, stirring constantly. Stir in water; cook and stir 30 to 45 seconds or until slightly thickened. Add banana and rum extract, stirring gently to coat in caramel mixture. Cook about 30 seconds or until banana is heated through.

3. Scoop ice cream into four individual dessert dishes; spoon banana mixture over ice cream. Garnish with wafer cookie pieces. Serve immediately.

Makes 4 servings

Nutrients per Serving (½ cup ice cream with 2 tablespoons topping): Calories: 172, Calories from Fat: 21%, Total Fat: 4g, Saturated Fat: 2g, Cholesterol: 15mg, Sodium: 71mg, Carbohydrate: 30g, Fiber: 2g, Protein: 3g

Tip Brown sugar is an important ingredient in this recipe because it gives the dish a deeper, richer flavor. Unfortunately, it dries out very quickly in the pantry and becomes hard and lumpy. To soften, place the brown sugar in a microwavable bowl. Cover with plastic wrap; microwave on HIGH 30 seconds. Stir and repeat if needed.

•Cool & Creamy•

Mocha Cappuccino Ice Cream Pie

$1/4$ **cup cold water**
1 **tablespoon instant coffee granules**
4 **packets sugar substitute *or* equivalent of 8 teaspoons sugar**
$1/2$ **teaspoon vanilla**
4 **cups fudge marble fat-free sugar-free ice cream, slightly softened**
1 **vanilla wafer pie crust**
Thawed fat-free whipped topping (optional)

1. Combine water, coffee granules, sugar substitute and vanilla in small bowl; stir until coffee granules dissolve.

2. Combine ice cream and coffee mixture in large bowl; stir until well blended. Spoon into pie crust; smooth top.

3. Cover and freeze about 4 hours or until firm. Garnish with whipped topping.

Makes 8 servings

Variation: Omit pie crust and serve filling in dessert cups with biscotti.

Nutrients per Serving: Calories: 201, Calories from Fat: 34%, Total Fat: 8g, Saturated Fat: 2g, Cholesterol: 9mg, Sodium: 159mg, Carbohydrate: 29g, Fiber: 0g, Protein: 5g

Tip Substitute $1/4$ cup cold very strong coffee for the water and instant coffee granules.

No-Bake Pumpkin Mousse Parfaits

    2 ounces reduced-fat cream cheese, softened
    1 can (15 ounces) solid-pack pumpkin
 ³/₄ cup fat-free (skim) milk
    1 package (4-serving size) vanilla fat-free sugar-free instant pudding
        and pie filling mix
    1 teaspoon ground cinnamon
 ¹/₂ teaspoon ground ginger
 ¹/₈ teaspoon ground cloves
    3 cups thawed reduced-fat whipped topping, divided
    4 gingersnap cookies, crushed

1. Beat cream cheese in medium bowl with electric mixer at medium speed until smooth. Add pumpkin, milk, pudding mix, cinnamon, ginger and cloves; beat 1 minute or until smooth. Fold in 1¹/₂ cups whipped topping.

2. Spoon ¹/₄ cup mousse into each of eight 6-ounce dessert glasses. Spoon 2 tablespoons whipped topping over mousse in each glass. Top with ¹/₄ cup mousse. Cover and refrigerate 1 hour.

3. Just before serving, top each parfait with remaining whipped topping and gingersnap crumbs. *Makes 8 servings*

Nutrients per Serving: Calories: 138, Calories from Fat: 39%, Total Fat: 6g, Saturated Fat: 3g, Cholesterol: 5mg, Sodium: 249mg, Carbohydrate: 19g, Fiber: 2g, Protein: 3g

• Cool & Creamy •

Strawberry Sundae Pie

¼ cup creamy peanut butter
3 tablespoons light corn syrup
2 cups crisp rice cereal
1¾ cups chocolate no-sugar-added fat-free frozen yogurt, slightly softened
1½ cups strawberry or raspberry fat-free sorbet
Sliced fresh strawberries (optional)

1. Spray 9-inch pie pan with nonstick cooking spray. Combine peanut butter and corn syrup in medium bowl; stir until blended. Stir in cereal until coated. Press onto bottom and up side of prepared pie pan. Loosely cover and refrigerate 15 minutes.

2. Gently spread frozen yogurt in crust. Use small ice cream scoop to scoop sorbet into small balls onto yogurt layer. Cover and freeze about 2 hours or until firm.

3. Let pie stand at room temperature 10 minutes. Garnish with sliced strawberries.

Makes 9 servings

Nutrients per Serving: Calories: 154, Calories from Fat: 23%, Total Fat: 4g, Saturated Fat: <1g, Cholesterol: 1mg, Sodium: 111mg, Carbohydrate: 27g, Fiber: <1g, Protein: 4g

Berries with Banana Cream

162
calories

⅓ cup reduced-fat sour cream
½ small ripe banana, cut into chunks
1 tablespoon frozen orange juice concentrate
2 cups sliced fresh strawberries, blueberries, raspberries or a combination
⅛ teaspoon ground cinnamon or nutmeg

1. Combine sour cream, banana and orange juice concentrate in blender; blend until smooth.

2. Place berries in two serving dishes. Top with sour cream mixture; sprinkle with cinnamon.

Makes 2 servings

Nutrients per Serving (1 cup berries with about 3 tablespoons sour cream mixture): Calories: 162, Calories from Fat: 29%, Total Fat: 6g, Saturated Fat: 3g, Cholesterol: 20mg, Sodium: 26mg, Carbohydrate: 27g, Fiber: 6g, Protein: 3g

•300 Calorie•
Contents

·Beef· & Pork

Retro Beef and Veggie Soup Stew

3 teaspoons olive oil, divided
3/4 pound beef top sirloin steak, cut into bite-size pieces
2 medium carrots, quartered lengthwise and cut into 2-inch pieces
1 medium green bell pepper, coarsely chopped
6 ounces green beans, cut into 2-inch pieces
1 can (about 14 ounces) Italian-style stewed tomatoes
1 cup beef broth
8 ounces new potatoes, cut into bite-size pieces
3 teaspoons instant coffee granules, divided
2 tablespoons all-purpose flour
3/4 teaspoon salt
1/4 teaspoon black pepper

1. Heat 1 teaspoon oil in Dutch oven over medium-high heat. Brown beef 1 to 2 minutes; transfer to plate.

2. Add remaining 2 teaspoons oil, carrots, bell pepper and green beans to Dutch oven. Cook and stir 4 minutes or until edges begin to brown. Add tomatoes, broth, potatoes and 1 teaspoon coffee granules; bring to a boil. Reduce heat. Add beef; cover and simmer 20 minutes or until potatoes are tender.

3. Stir in remaining 2 teaspoons coffee granules, flour, salt and black pepper. Cook, uncovered, 10 to 15 minutes or until thickened.   *Makes 4 servings*

Nutrients per Serving: Calories: 265, Calories from Fat: 23%, Total Fat: 7g, Saturated Fat: 2g, Cholesterol: 31mg, Sodium: 589mg, Carbohydrate: 28g, Fiber: 5g, Protein: 23g

• Beef **& Pork** •

Pork with Spicy Orange Cranberry Sauce

1 teaspoon chili powder
$1/2$ teaspoon ground cumin
$1/4$ teaspoon ground allspice
$1/4$ teaspoon salt
$1/4$ teaspoon black pepper
4 boneless pork chops (about 1 pound)
1 tablespoon canola oil
1 cup whole-berry cranberry sauce
$1/2$ teaspoon grated orange peel
$1/4$ teaspoon ground cinnamon
$1/8$ teaspoon red pepper flakes

1. Combine chili powder, cumin, allspice, salt and black pepper in small bowl; mix well. Sprinkle over both sides of pork chops.

2. Heat oil in large nonstick skillet over medium heat. Add pork; cook 4 to 5 minutes per side or until barely pink in center.

3. Combine cranberry sauce, orange peel, cinnamon and red pepper flakes in small bowl; mix well. Serve sauce with pork chops. *Makes 4 servings*

Nutrients per Serving: Calories: 276, Calories from Fat: 28%, Total Fat: 9g, Saturated Fat: 2g, Cholesterol: 51mg, Sodium: 204mg, Carbohydrate: 28g, Fiber: 2g, Protein: 20g

Pork with Spicy Orange Cranberry Sauce

• Beef & Pork •

Butternut Gratin

- **1 butternut squash (about 1¾ pounds)**
- **6 ounces boneless pork chops, trimmed of fat, cooked and cut into bite-size pieces**
- **½ cup chopped celery**
- **⅓ cup whole grain bread crumbs**
- **¼ cup sliced green onions**
- **¼ cup vegetable broth**
- **2 tablespoons shredded reduced-fat Cheddar cheese**
- **¼ teaspoon black pepper (optional)**

Microwave Directions

1. Pierce squash with tip of knife in several places. Microwave on HIGH 8 to 9 minutes or until squash is almost tender.

2. Let squash stand about 5 minutes or until cool enough to handle. Cut off ends and discard. Cut squash in half lengthwise; remove and discard seeds. Use knife to score each half into grid of 1-inch cubes, leaving skin intact. Cut cubes from skin.

3. Spray 1-to 1½-quart microwavable dish with nonstick cooking spray. Combine 2 cups squash cubes, pork, celery, bread crumbs, green onions and broth in prepared dish. Sprinkle with cheese. Microwave on HIGH 2 to 2½ minutes or until squash is tender and mixture is heated through. Season with pepper, if desired.

Makes 2 servings

Tip: Acorn squash can be substituted.

Nutrients per Serving (1¾ cups): Calories: 285, Calories from Fat: 25%, Total Fat: 8g, Saturated Fat: 3g, Cholesterol: 83mg, Sodium: 452mg, Carbohydrate: 23g, Fiber: 5g, Protein: 31g

• Beef **& Pork** •

Beef Brisket

1 large onion, thinly sliced
1 small (2 to 2$\frac{1}{2}$ pounds) well-trimmed beef brisket
$\frac{1}{2}$ teaspoon salt
$\frac{1}{2}$ teaspoon black pepper
$\frac{2}{3}$ cup chili sauce, divided
1$\frac{1}{2}$ tablespoons brown sugar
$\frac{1}{4}$ teaspoon ground cinnamon
2 large sweet potatoes, peeled and cut into 1-inch pieces
1 cup (5 ounces) pitted prunes
2 tablespoons cornstarch
2 tablespoons cold water

Slow Cooker Directions

1. Place onion in slow cooker. Arrange brisket over onion (tucking edges under to fit, if necessary). Sprinkle with salt and pepper; top with $\frac{1}{3}$ cup chili sauce. Cover; cook on HIGH 3$\frac{1}{2}$ hours.

2. Combine remaining $\frac{1}{3}$ cup chili sauce, brown sugar and cinnamon in large bowl. Add sweet potatoes and prunes; toss to coat. Spoon mixture over brisket. Cover; cook on HIGH 1$\frac{1}{4}$ to 1$\frac{1}{2}$ hours or until brisket and sweet potatoes are tender.

3. Transfer brisket to cutting board; tent with foil. Transfer sweet potato mixture to serving platter, leaving juices in slow cooker. Keep warm.

4. Blend cornstarch into water in small bowl until smooth. Stir mixture into slow cooker juices. Cover; cook on HIGH 10 minutes or until sauce thickens.

5. Cut brisket crosswise into thin slices. Serve with sweet potato mixture and sauce.

Makes 8 servings

Nutrients per Serving: Calories: 284, Calories from Fat: 22%, Total Fat: 7g, Saturated Fat: 2g, Cholesterol: 68mg, Sodium: 523mg, Carbohydrate: 30g, Fiber: 4g, Protein: 25g

Easy Pork Puttanesca

6 ounces uncooked whole wheat spaghetti
¹/₂ pound pork tenderloin, cut into bite-size pieces
¹/₄ teaspoon black pepper
1 jar (24 ounces) tomato-basil pasta sauce
¹/₂ cup (2 ounces) pitted and coarsely chopped kalamata olives
1 tablespoon capers, drained (optional)
¹/₄ teaspoon fennel seeds, crushed
¹/₈ teaspoon red pepper flakes
¹/₄ cup grated Parmesan cheese
2 tablespoons chopped fresh basil

1. Cook spaghetti according to package directions, omitting salt and fat. Drain and keep warm.

2. Spray large nonstick skillet with nonstick cooking spray; heat over medium-high heat. Add pork; sprinkle with black pepper. Cook and stir 2 to 3 minutes or until lightly browned.

3. Stir in pasta sauce, olives, capers, if desired, fennel seeds and red pepper flakes. Bring to a boil. Reduce heat; simmer about 2 minutes or until pork is cooked through.

4. Arrange spaghetti on serving plates. Top with pork mixture. Sprinkle with Parmesan and basil. *Makes 4 servings*

Nutrients per Serving: Calories: 303, Calories from Fat: 15%, Total Fat: 5g, Saturated Fat: 1g, Cholesterol: 38mg, Sodium: 742mg, Carbohydrate: 45g, Fiber: 3g, Protein: 22g

•Beef & Pork•

Sirloin Steak Antipasto Salad

  3 cloves garlic, minced
$^1/_2$ teaspoon black pepper
  1 beef top sirloin steak (about 1 pound and $^3/_4$ inch thick), trimmed of fat
  8 cups torn romaine lettuce
16 cherry tomatoes, halved
16 pitted kalamata olives, halved lengthwise
  1 can (14 ounces) quartered artichoke hearts, drained
$^1/_3$ cup fat-free Italian or Caesar salad dressing
$^1/_4$ cup fresh basil, cut into thin strips

1. Prepare grill for direct cooking or preheat broiler. Sprinkle garlic and pepper over steak.

2. Grill steak over medium-hot coals or broil 4 inches from heat 4 minutes per side for medium-rare doneness or until desired doneness. Transfer steak to cutting board; tent with foil. Let stand at least 5 minutes.

3. Meanwhile, combine lettuce, tomatoes, olives and artichoke hearts in large bowl. Add dressing; toss well. Transfer to four plates.

4. Cut steak crosswise into thin slices; arrange over salads. Drizzle juices from cutting board over steak. Sprinkle with basil.   *Makes 4 servings*

Nutrients per Serving: Calories: 250, Calories from Fat: 23%, Total Fat: 7g, Saturated Fat: 2g, Cholesterol: 53mg, Sodium: 776mg, Carbohydrate: 21g, Fiber: 9g, Protein: 30g

Tip   Beef top sirloin steak is a versatile cut of meat that can be grilled, broiled or cooked in a skillet. When cooking steaks, use a spatula or tongs to prevent the loss of meat juices.

Sirloin Steak Antipasto Salad

• Beef & Pork •

Pork and Toasted Peanut Toss

1 packet boil-in-bag rice *or* **1 cup uncooked instant rice**
¼ cup plus 2 tablespoons unsalted dry-roasted peanuts
½ pound pork tenderloin, cut into thin strips
3 tablespoons cider vinegar
3 tablespoons reduced-sodium soy sauce
2 tablespoons water
4 packets sugar substitute*
2 teaspoons grated fresh ginger
⅛ teaspoon salt
⅛ teaspoon red pepper flakes
1 medium onion, cut into 8 wedges
1 large green bell pepper, thinly sliced
1 medium carrot, cut into thin strips

*This recipe was tested with sucralose-based sugar substitute.

1. Cook rice according to package directions, omitting salt and fat. Set aside.

2. Cook peanuts in medium skillet over medium-high heat, stirring constantly, 3 minutes or until lightly browned. Remove to plate.

3. Spray skillet with nonstick cooking spray. Add pork; cook and stir 3 minutes or until no longer pink. Remove to plate.

4. Combine vinegar, soy sauce, water, sugar substitute, ginger, salt and red pepper flakes in small saucepan; stir until well blended. Heat over medium heat until warm.

5. Spray skillet with cooking spray. Add onion, bell pepper and carrot; cook and stir 4 minutes or until crisp-tender. Add peanuts and pork to skillet; cook and stir 1 minute.

6. Serve pork mixture over rice; top with sauce.   *Makes 4 servings*

Nutrients per Serving: Calories: 285, Calories from Fat: 28%, Total Fat: 9g, Saturated Fat: 2g, Cholesterol: 37mg, Sodium: 495mg, Carbohydrate: 34g, Fiber: 3g, Protein: 19g

Beef & Pork

Fajita Pile-Ups

2 teaspoons vegetable oil, divided
$^3/_4$ pound beef top sirloin steak, trimmed of fat, cut into thin strips
2 teaspoons salt-free steak seasoning
$^1/_2$ medium lime
1 medium green bell pepper, cut into $^1/_2$-inch strips
1 medium red or yellow bell pepper, cut into $^1/_2$-inch strips
1 large onion, cut into $^1/_2$-inch wedges
1 cup cherry tomatoes, halved
$^1/_2$ teaspoon ground cumin
4 (6-inch) corn tortillas
$^1/_2$ cup fat-free sour cream
2 tablespoons chopped fresh cilantro (optional)
Lime wedges (optional)

1. Heat 1 teaspoon oil in large nonstick skillet over medium-high heat. Add steak; sprinkle with seasoning. Cook and stir 3 minutes or until slightly pink in center. *Do not overcook.* Transfer to plate. Squeeze $^1/_2$ lime over steak. Cover to keep warm.

2. Add remaining 1 teaspoon oil to skillet. Add bell peppers and onion; cook and stir 8 minutes or until tender. Add tomatoes; cook and stir 1 minute. Return steak with any accumulated juices and cumin to skillet; cook and stir 1 minute.

3. Warm tortillas according to package directions. Top tortillas evenly with steak mixture. Serve with sour cream; garnish with cilantro and lime wedges.

Makes 4 servings

Nutrients per Serving: Calories: 252, Calories from Fat: 24%, Total Fat: 7g, Saturated Fat: 2g, Cholesterol: 41mg, Sodium: 90mg, Carbohydrate: 24g, Fiber: 4g, Protein: 24g

Fajita Pile-Ups

• Beef & Pork •

Old-Fashioned Meat Loaf

1 teaspoon olive oil
1 cup finely chopped onion
4 cloves garlic, minced
1½ pounds extra-lean ground beef
1 cup chili sauce, divided
¾ cup old-fashioned oats
2 egg whites
½ teaspoon black pepper
¼ teaspoon salt (optional)
1 tablespoon Dijon mustard

1. Preheat oven to 375°F. Heat oil in large nonstick skillet over medium heat. Add onion; cook and stir 5 minutes. Add garlic; cook and stir 1 minute. Transfer to large bowl; cool 5 minutes.

2. Add beef, ½ cup chili sauce, oats, egg whites, pepper and salt, if desired, to bowl; mix well. Pat into 9×5-inch loaf pan. Combine remaining ½ cup chili sauce and mustard in small bowl; spoon evenly over top of meat loaf.

3. Bake 45 to 50 minutes or until cooked through (160°F). Let stand 5 minutes. Pour off any juices from pan. Cut into slices. *Makes 6 servings*

Nutrients per Serving: Calories: 263, Calories from Fat: 26%, Total Fat: 7g, Saturated Fat: 3g, Cholesterol: 70mg, Sodium: 690mg, Carbohydrate: 18g, Fiber: 4g, Protein: 28g

Old-Fashioned Meat Loaf

263 calories

Steak and Mushroom Skewers

¼ cup fat-free Italian salad dressing
2 tablespoons Worcestershire sauce
¾ pound beef top sirloin steak, cut into 24 (1-inch) cubes
24 medium whole mushrooms (about 12 ounces)
¼ cup light mayonnaise
¼ cup fat-free sour cream
1 clove garlic, minced
¼ to ½ teaspoon dried rosemary
¼ teaspoon salt
1 medium zucchini, cut into 24 (1-inch) pieces
1 medium green bell pepper, cut into 24 (1-inch) pieces

1. Combine salad dressing and Worcestershire sauce in small bowl. Reserve 2 tablespoons dressing mixture. Combine beef, mushrooms and remaining dressing mixture in large resealable food storage bag. Seal bag; turn to coat. Marinate in refrigerator 30 to 60 minutes.

2. For sauce, combine mayonnaise, sour cream, garlic, rosemary and salt in small bowl. Cover and refrigerate until ready to serve.

3. Prepare grill for direct cooking. Thread eight 10-inch skewers, alternating beef, mushrooms, zucchini and bell pepper. Discard remaining marinade.

4. Grill 6 to 8 minutes over medium-high heat or until desired doneness, turning occasionally. *Do not overcook.* Before serving, brush with reserved 2 tablespoons dressing mixture. Serve with sauce. *Makes 4 servings*

Nutrients per Serving (2 skewers with 2 tablespoons sauce): Calories: 263, Calories from Fat: 31%, Total Fat: 10g, Saturated Fat: 2g, Cholesterol: 59mg, Sodium: 544mg, Carbohydrate: 24g, Fiber: 3g, Protein: 24g

Steak and Mushroom Skewers

Spanish-Style Pork with Mango Salsa

2 teaspoons canola oil

$^3/_4$ cup coarsely chopped onion

2 cloves garlic, minced

$^3/_4$ pound pork tenderloin, cut into 1-inch cubes

1 teaspoon ground cinnamon

1 teaspoon ground cumin

1 teaspoon dried oregano

$^1/_2$ teaspoon ground coriander

$^1/_4$ teaspoon salt

1 medium mango, peeled and cut into bite-size pieces (about 1$^1/_2$ cups)

1 cup chunky salsa

2 cups cooked brown rice

2 tablespoons slivered almonds, toasted (optional)

1. Heat oil in large nonstick skillet over medium-high heat. Add onion; cook and stir 4 minutes or until tender. Add garlic; cook and stir 30 seconds. Add pork, cinnamon, cumin, oregano, coriander and salt; cook and stir 5 to 6 minutes or until pork is well browned on all sides.

2. Reduce heat to medium-low. Stir in mango and salsa. Cover and cook 3 to 4 minutes or until heated through. Serve over rice. Sprinkle with almonds, if desired.

Makes 4 servings

Nutrients per Serving: Calories: 309, Calories from Fat: 14%, Total Fat: 5g, Saturated Fat: 1g, Cholesterol: 55mg, Sodium: 510mg, Carbohydrate: 43g, Fiber: 4g, Protein: 21g

Spanish-Style Pork with Mango Salsa

• Beef **& Pork** •

Taco-Topped Potatoes

4 red or Yukon Gold potatoes (about 6 ounces each), scrubbed and pierced with fork

$^1/_2$ pound 96% lean ground beef

$^1/_2$ (1$^1/_4$-ounce) package taco seasoning mix

$^1/_2$ cup water

1 cup diced tomatoes

$^1/_4$ teaspoon salt

2 cups shredded lettuce

$^1/_2$ cup (2 ounces) shredded reduced-fat sharp Cheddar cheese

$^1/_4$ cup finely chopped green onions

$^1/_2$ cup fat-free sour cream

1. Microwave potatoes on HIGH 6 to 7 minutes or until fork-tender.

2. Brown beef in large nonstick skillet over medium-high heat 6 to 8 minutes, stirring to break up meat. Drain fat. Add seasoning mix and water; stir to blend. Cook 1 minute. Remove from heat.

3. Toss tomatoes with salt in medium bowl.

4. Split potatoes almost in half and fluff with fork. Fill with beef mixture, tomatoes, lettuce, cheese and green onions. Serve with sour cream.   *Makes 4 servings*

Nutrients per Serving: Calories 307, Calories from Fat: 36%, Total Fat: 12g, Saturated Fat: 5g, Cholesterol: 53mg, Sodium: 759mg, Carbohydrate: 29g, Fiber: 3g, Protein: 19g

Taco-Topped Potato

Pork Chops and Stuffing Skillet Casserole

4 thin bone-in pork chops (1 pound)
¼ teaspoon dried thyme
¼ teaspoon paprika
⅛ teaspoon salt
¼ pound 50%-less-fat bulk pork sausage
2 cups corn bread stuffing mix
1 cup frozen diced green bell peppers, thawed
⅛ to ¼ teaspoon poultry seasoning (optional)
1¼ cups water

1. Preheat oven to 350°F. Sprinkle one side of pork chops with thyme, paprika and salt. Spray large ovenproof skillet with nonstick cooking spray; heat over medium-high heat. Add pork, seasoned side down; cook 2 minutes. Remove to plate.

2. Add sausage to skillet; cook until no longer pink, stirring to break up meat. Remove from heat; stir in stuffing mix, bell peppers, poultry seasoning, if desired, and water just until blended.

3. Arrange pork, seasoned side up, over stuffing mixture. Cover and bake 15 minutes or until pork is no longer pink in center. Let stand 5 minutes before serving.

Makes 4 servings

Nutrients per Serving: Calories: 305, Calories from Fat: 44%, Total Fat: 14g, Saturated Fat: 5g, Cholesterol: 92mg, Sodium: 499mg, Carbohydrate: 13g, Fiber: 3g, Protein: 28g

·Chicken·
& Turkey

Grilled Chipotle Chicken Sandwiches

  1 **medium lime, halved**
  4 **boneless skinless chicken breasts (4 ounces each), flattened slightly**
$\frac{1}{2}$ **cup fat-free sour cream**
  2 **tablespoons light mayonnaise**
  1 **canned chipotle pepper in adobo sauce**
  2 **teaspoons adobo sauce from canned chipotle**
$\frac{1}{8}$ **teaspoon salt (optional)**
   Black pepper
  2 **slices Swiss cheese, cut in half diagonally**
  4 **whole wheat hamburger buns, split**
  4 **leaves romaine lettuce**
  4 **thin slices red onion**

1. Squeeze juice from half of lime evenly over chicken. Spray grill grid with nonstick cooking spray. Prepare grill for direct cooking.

2. Combine sour cream, mayonnaise, chipotle pepper, adobo sauce and salt, if desired, in food processor or blender; process until smooth.

3. Grill chicken over medium-high heat 10 minutes. Turn and sprinkle with black pepper. Grill 10 minutes or until chicken is no longer pink in center. Move chicken to side of grill. Squeeze remaining lime half over chicken; top with cheese.

4. Place cut sides of buns on grill; toast lightly. Spread with chipotle mixture. Arrange lettuce, chicken and onion on bun bottoms; cover with bun tops.

Makes 4 servings

Nutrients per Serving: Calories: 299, Calories from Fat: 24%, Total Fat: 8g, Saturated Fat: 3g, Cholesterol: 82mg, Sodium: 798mg, Carbohydrate: 22g, Fiber: 3g, Protein: 33g

• Chicken **& Turkey** •

Turkey Stroganoff

2 cups sliced mushrooms

1 stalk celery, thinly sliced

1 medium shallot *or* 1/4 small onion, minced

1/2 cup reduced-sodium chicken broth

1/4 teaspoon dried thyme

1/8 teaspoon black pepper

1 turkey tenderloin or turkey breast, cut into bite-size pieces

1/4 cup fat-free sour cream

2 teaspoons all-purpose flour

1/8 teaspoon salt (optional)

2/3 cup cooked wide cholesterol-free whole wheat egg noodles

Slow Cooker Directions

1. Spray large skillet with nonstick cooking spray. Add mushrooms, celery and shallot; cook and stir over medium heat 5 minutes or until mushrooms and shallot are tender. Spoon into small slow cooker. Stir in broth, thyme and pepper. Stir in turkey. Cover; cook on LOW 5 to 6 hours.

2. Combine sour cream and flour in small bowl. Spoon 2 tablespoons liquid from slow cooker into bowl; stir well. Stir sour cream mixture into slow cooker. Cover; cook 10 minutes. Stir in salt, if desired.

3. Spoon noodles onto serving plates. Top with turkey mixture.   *Makes 2 servings*

Nutrients per Serving (1 cup turkey mixture with 1/3 cup noodles): Calories: 310, Calories from Fat: 9%, Total Fat: 3g, Saturated Fat: 1g, Cholesterol: 100mg, Sodium: 123mg, Carbohydrate: 41g, Fiber: 3g, Protein: 30g

• Chicken & Turkey •

Chicken Salad Pitas

4 cups torn mixed spring greens
2 cups chopped cooked chicken breast
¹/₂ cup chopped green bell pepper or poblano pepper
¹/₂ cup reduced-fat ranch salad dressing
4 whole wheat pita bread rounds, halved crosswise
    Black pepper (optional)

1. Toss greens, chicken, bell pepper and salad dressing in large bowl. Microwave pita halves on HIGH 12 to 15 seconds.

2. Fill each warmed pita half with salad mixture. Sprinkle with black pepper, if desired. *Makes 4 servings*

Nutrients per Serving: Calories: 325, Calories from Fat: 11%, Total Fat: 4g, Saturated Fat: <1g, Cholesterol: 54mg, Sodium: 561mg, Carbohydrate: 44g, Fiber: 6g, Protein: 29g

Chicken Couscous

¹/₂ pound boneless skinless chicken breasts, cut into 1-inch cubes
4 medium zucchini, sliced
1 can (about 14 ounces) diced tomatoes
1 can (about 14 ounces) fat-free reduced-sodium chicken broth
1 teaspoon Italian seasoning
1 cup uncooked whole wheat couscous

1. Spray large skillet with nonstick cooking spray; heat over medium-high heat. Cook and stir chicken 4 minutes or until lightly browned.

2. Add zucchini, tomatoes, broth and Italian seasoning. Reduce heat to low; simmer 15 minutes, stirring occasionally.

3. Stir in couscous; remove from heat. Cover and let stand 7 minutes. Fluff with fork. *Makes 4 servings*

Nutrients per Serving: Calories: 278, Calories from Fat: 4%, Total Fat: 1g, Saturated Fat: <1g, Cholesterol: 33mg, Sodium: 322mg, Carbohydrate: 44g, Fiber: 5g, Protein: 22g

Chicken Salad Pitas

Southwestern Chicken and Black Bean Skillet

1 teaspoon ground cumin
1 teaspoon chili powder
1/2 teaspoon salt
4 boneless skinless chicken breasts (about 1 pound)
2 teaspoons canola oil
1 cup chopped onion
1 red bell pepper, chopped
1 can (about 15 ounces) black beans, rinsed and drained
1/2 cup chunky salsa
1/4 cup chopped fresh cilantro or thinly sliced green onions (optional)

1. Combine cumin, chili powder and salt in small bowl; sprinkle over both sides of chicken.

2. Heat oil in large nonstick skillet over medium-high heat. Add chicken; cook 4 minutes, turning once. Remove to plate.

3. Add onion to same skillet; cook and stir 1 minute. Add bell pepper; cook 5 minutes, stirring occasionally. Stir in beans and salsa.

4. Place chicken on top of bean mixture. Cover and cook 6 to 7 minutes or until chicken is no longer pink in center. Garnish with cilantro.   *Makes 4 servings*

Nutrients per Serving: Calories: 262, Calories from Fat: 14%, Total Fat: 4g, Saturated Fat: <1g, Cholesterol: 66mg, Sodium: 528mg, Carbohydrate: 22g, Fiber: 7g, Protein: 33g

Southwestern Chicken and Black Bean Skillet

• Chicken & Turkey •

Turkey Piccata

3 tablespoons all-purpose flour
¼ teaspoon salt
¼ teaspoon black pepper
2 egg whites
1 teaspoon water
⅔ cup plain dry bread crumbs
1 package (about 17½ ounces) turkey breast cutlets or slices
3 teaspoons butter, divided
3 teaspoons olive oil, divided
2 cloves garlic, minced
¾ to 1 cup fat-free reduced-sodium chicken broth
2 tablespoons capers, rinsed and drained
2 tablespoons lemon juice
2 tablespoons chopped fresh parsley
1 teaspoon grated lemon peel

1. Combine flour, salt and pepper in small resealable food storage bag. Beat egg whites and water in small shallow bowl. Place bread crumbs on small shallow plate. Add one cutlet to bag; shake to coat lightly with flour mixture. Dip cutlet in egg mixture; let excess drip off. Roll in bread crumbs; press each side to coat. Repeat with remaining cutlets. Discard any remaining flour, egg and crumb mixture.

2. Heat 1 teaspoon butter and 1 teaspoon oil in large nonstick skillet over medium heat. Add half of cutlets; cook about 3 minutes per side or until golden brown and no longer pink in center. Remove to plate and keep warm. Repeat with 1 teaspoon butter, 1 teaspoon oil and remaining cutlets.

3. Heat remaining 1 teaspoon butter and 1 teaspoon oil in same skillet. Add garlic; cook 1 minute. Stir in broth, capers and lemon juice; simmer 1 to 2 minutes or until sauce is slightly reduced. Pour sauce over cutlets; sprinkle with parsley and lemon peel. *Makes 4 servings*

Nutrients per Serving (2 cutlets): Calories: 296, Calories from Fat: 27%, Total Fat: 9g, Saturated Fat: 3g, Cholesterol: 59mg, Sodium: 551mg, Carbohydrate: 19g, Fiber: 1g, Protein: 34g

Turkey Piccata

•Chicken **& Turkey**•

Lettuce Wrap Enchiladas

2 bell peppers, cut into ¼-inch strips
2 tablespoons water
½ tablespoon chili powder
1 cup shredded or cubed cooked chicken
½ cup fresh cilantro, chopped
4 leaves romaine lettuce
½ cup canned fat-free reduced-sodium refried beans, warmed
½ cup salsa
½ cup (2 ounces) shredded reduced-fat Cheddar cheese
¼ cup fat-free sour cream

1. Spray large skillet with nonstick cooking spray; heat over medium-high heat. Add bell peppers, water and chili powder; cook 4 to 5 minutes or until water evaporates, stirring occasionally. Reduce heat to low. Add chicken; heat until warm. Stir in cilantro; cover and keep warm.

2. Fill each lettuce leaf with one fourth of beans and one fourth of chicken mixture. Top with salsa, cheese and sour cream. *Makes 2 servings*

Nutrients per Serving (2 wraps): Calories: 290, Calories from Fat: 28%, Total Fat: 9g, Saturated Fat: 4g, Cholesterol: 79mg, Sodium: 651mg, Carbohydrate: 21g, Fiber: 6g, Protein: 33g

Skillet Lasagna with Vegetables

$^1/_2$ pound hot Italian turkey sausage, casing removed

$^1/_2$ pound 93% lean ground turkey

2 stalks celery, sliced

$^1/_3$ cup chopped onion

2 cups marinara sauce

1$^1/_3$ cups water

4 ounces uncooked bowtie pasta

1 medium zucchini, halved lengthwise and cut into $^1/_2$-inch-thick slices (2 cups)

$^3/_4$ cup chopped green or yellow bell pepper

$^1/_2$ cup reduced-fat ricotta cheese

2 tablespoons finely shredded Parmesan cheese

$^1/_2$ cup (2 ounces) shredded part-skim mozzarella cheese

1. Cook and stir sausage, turkey, celery and onion in large skillet over medium-high heat until turkey is no longer pink. Stir in marinara sauce and water. Bring to a boil. Add pasta; stir. Reduce heat to medium-low; cover and simmer 12 minutes.

2. Stir in zucchini and bell pepper; cover and simmer 2 minutes. Uncover and simmer 4 to 6 minutes or until vegetables are crisp-tender.

3. Meanwhile, combine ricotta and Parmesan in small bowl. Drop by rounded teaspoonfuls on top of mixture in skillet. Sprinkle with mozzarella. Remove from heat; cover and let stand 10 minutes. *Makes 6 servings*

Nutrients per Serving: Calories: 300, Calories from Fat: 33%, Total Fat: 11g, Saturated Fat: 2.5g, Cholesterol: 45mg, Sodium: 750mg, Carbohydrate: 24g, Fiber: 3g, Protein: 25g

• Chicken **& Turkey** •

Quick Chicken Sausage Jambalaya

1 pouch (about 9 ounces) ready-to-serve brown rice
2 teaspoons canola oil
1 cup chopped onion
1 small green bell pepper, diced
3 cloves garlic, minced
2 tablespoons all-purpose flour
1 can (about 14 ounces) diced fire-roasted tomatoes
1 cup reduced-sodium chicken broth
1 package (9 ounces) fully cooked spicy chicken or andouille sausage, cut into $1/2$-inch-thick slices
1 teaspoon dried thyme
$1/4$ teaspoon hot pepper sauce or smoked hot pepper sauce (optional)
   Red chiles and sliced green onions (optional)

1. Cook rice according to package directions.

2. Heat oil in large saucepan over medium heat. Add onion, bell pepper and garlic; cook 5 minutes, stirring occasionally. Stir in flour; cook and stir 1 minute. Add tomatoes, broth, sausage, thyme and hot pepper sauce, if desired. Bring to a boil over high heat. Reduce heat to low; simmer, uncovered, 15 minutes or until vegetables are tender and sauce thickens.

3. Stir in rice or serve over rice. Garnish with red chiles and green onions.

Makes 4 servings

Nutrients per Serving: Calories: 291, Calories from Fat: 22%, Total Fat: 7g, Saturated Fat: 1g, Cholesterol: 54mg, Sodium: 511mg, Carbohydrate: 38g, Fiber: 4g, Protein: 19g

Quick Chicken Sausage Jambalaya

• Chicken & Turkey •

Turkey Sliders

1 pound extra-lean ground turkey
¼ cup finely chopped green onions
2 tablespoons low-fat mayonnaise
1 tablespoon Worcestershire sauce
¼ teaspoon black pepper
⅛ teaspoon salt
12 baby spinach leaves
¼ cup (1 ounce) shredded reduced-fat sharp Cheddar cheese
1 shallot, thinly cut into 12 slices
1 tablespoon steak sauce (optional)
12 mini whole wheat pita bread rounds, cut in half horizontally

1. Combine turkey, green onions, mayonnaise, Worcestershire sauce, pepper and salt in large bowl; mix lightly. Shape into 12 (2-inch) patties.

2. Spray large nonstick skillet with nonstick cooking spray; heat over medium heat. Add patties; cook 5 minutes per side or until cooked through.

3. Arrange spinach, turkey patty, cheese, shallot and steak sauce, if desired, on pita bottoms. Cover with pita tops. *Makes 6 servings*

Nutrients per Serving (2 sliders): Calories: 262, Calories from Fat: 14%, Total Fat: 4g, Saturated Fat: 1g, Cholesterol: 43mg, Sodium: 596mg, Carbohydrate: 31g, Fiber: 2g, Protein: 24g

• Chicken & Turkey •

Roasted Pepper Picante Chicken

4 ounces uncooked yolk-free egg noodles
1 pound chicken tenders, cut into bite-size pieces
$^1/_2$ cup chopped roasted red peppers
$^1/_2$ cup mild or medium picante sauce
$^1/_4$ cup water
$^1/_2$ teaspoon ground cumin
$^3/_4$ cup (3 ounces) shredded reduced-fat sharp Cheddar cheese

1. Cook noodles according to package directions, omitting salt and fat. Drain.

2. Meanwhile, spray medium skillet with nonstick cooking spray; heat over medium-high heat. Add chicken; cook and stir 2 minutes. Add roasted peppers, picante sauce, water and cumin. Bring to a boil. Reduce heat to medium-low. Cover and simmer 10 minutes or until slightly thickened. Serve over noodles. Sprinkle with cheese.

Makes 4 servings

Nutrients per Serving: Calories: 314, Calories from Fat: 22%, Total Fat: 7g, Saturated Fat: 3g, Cholesterol: 114mg, Sodium: 513mg, Carbohydrate: 25g, Fiber: 1g, Protein: 35g

Chunky Chicken Stew

1 teaspoon olive oil
1 small onion, chopped
1 cup thinly sliced carrots
1 cup fat-free reduced-sodium chicken broth
1 can (about 14 ounces) no-salt-added diced tomatoes
1 cup diced cooked chicken breast
3 cups sliced kale or baby spinach

1. Heat oil in large saucepan over medium-high heat. Add onion; cook and stir 5 minutes or until golden brown. Stir in carrots and broth; bring to a boil. Reduce heat; simmer, uncovered, 5 minutes.

2. Stir in tomatoes; simmer 5 minutes or until carrots are tender. Add chicken; cook and stir until heated through. Add kale; stir until wilted. *Makes 2 servings*

Nutrients per Serving: Calories: 287, Calories from Fat: 18%, Total Fat: 6g, Saturated Fat: 1g, Cholesterol: 66mg, Sodium: 337mg, Carbohydrate: 30g, Fiber: 8g, Protein: 30g

Roasted Pepper Picante Chicken

• Chicken & Turkey •

Southwest Turkey Bake

1 pound extra-lean ground turkey
1 can (about 15 ounces) black beans, rinsed and drained
1 cup salsa
1/2 teaspoon ground cumin
1/8 teaspoon ground red pepper
1 package (81/2 ounces) corn muffin mix
3/4 cup reduced-sodium chicken broth
1 egg
3/4 cup (3 ounces) shredded reduced-fat Mexican cheese blend
Lime wedges (optional)

1. Preheat oven to 400°F. Brown turkey in large nonstick skillet over medium-high heat until no longer pink, stirring to break up meat. Stir in beans, salsa, cumin and red pepper; simmer 2 minutes.

2. Spoon turkey mixture into 13×9-inch baking dish.

3. Combine corn muffin mix, broth and egg in medium bowl; mix well. Spread over turkey mixture. Sprinkle evenly with cheese.

4. Bake 15 minutes or until edges are lightly browned. Serve with lime wedges, if desired. *Makes 8 servings*

Nutrients per Serving: Calories: 267, Calories from Fat: 24%, Total Fat: 7g, Saturated Fat: 2g, Cholesterol: 61mg, Sodium: 640mg, Carbohydrate: 29g, Fiber: 5g, Protein: 21g

Tip Extra-lean ground turkey is also known as ground turkey breast, which is the white meat of turkey and the lowest in fat of all ground turkey products. Because it is so lean, it can tend to dry out so it is best used in recipes when mixed with a liquid ingredient such as salsa.

Southwest Turkey Bake

Garden Pasta with Blue Cheese

6 ounces uncooked multigrain penne pasta
1 cup small fresh broccoli florets
1 medium carrot, thinly sliced
1 teaspoon canola oil
³/₄ pound boneless skinless chicken breasts, cut into thin strips
¹/₂ teaspoon dried thyme
¹/₂ medium red or orange bell pepper, thinly sliced
¹/₂ medium green bell pepper, thinly sliced
1¹/₂ ounces crumbled blue cheese
¹/₈ teaspoon black pepper

1. Cook pasta according to package directions, omitting salt and fat. Add broccoli and carrot during last 3 minutes of cooking.

2. Meanwhile, heat oil in large nonstick skillet over medium-high heat. Add chicken and thyme; cook and stir until chicken is cooked through. Remove to large bowl and keep warm.

3. Add bell peppers to skillet; cook and stir 4 minutes or until crisp-tender. Remove to same bowl and keep warm.

4. Drain pasta mixture, reserving ¹/₃ cup cooking water. Toss pasta mixture and reserved water with chicken and bell peppers. Add cheese and black pepper; stir gently. Cover and let stand 5 minutes before serving.   *Makes 4 servings*

Variation: Substitute rotini or spaghetti for the penne pasta.

Nutrients per Serving: Calories: 309, Calories from Fat: 18%, Total Fat: 6g, Saturated Fat: 2g, Cholesterol: 57mg, Sodium: 277mg, Carbohydrate: 33g, Fiber: 4g, Protein: 30g

Garden Pasta with Blue Cheese

• Chicken & Turkey •

Herb Roasted Turkey and Gravy

1/2 cup coarse-grain or Dijon mustard
1/4 cup chopped fresh sage
2 tablespoons chopped fresh thyme
2 tablespoons chopped fresh chives or tarragon
1 small (8- to 10-pound) turkey, thawed if frozen
2 tablespoons all-purpose flour
1 cup fat-free reduced-sodium chicken broth
1/4 cup fat-free half-and-half
1/4 teaspoon salt
1/4 teaspoon black pepper

1. Heat oven to 450°F. Combine mustard, sage, thyme and chives in small bowl.

2. Rinse turkey with cold water. Pat dry with paper towels. Carefully insert fingers under skin, beginning at neck cavity and sliding down over breast to form pocket between skin and turkey breast. Spoon mustard mixture into pocket. Use fingers to massage outside of skin, spreading mixture into even layer. Place turkey, breast side up, on rack in shallow roasting pan.

3. Place turkey in oven. *Reduce heat to 325°F.* Roast turkey 18 minutes per pound unstuffed (20 minutes per pound stuffed) or until internal temperature reads 165°F on meat thermometer inserted into thickest part of thigh not touching bone. Once turkey browns, tent with foil for remainder of roasting time. Transfer turkey to carving board; reserve pan drippings. Loosely tent turkey with foil; let stand 20 minutes before carving.

4. Meanwhile, pour reserved drippings from roasting pan into glass measuring cup. Spoon 2 tablespoons into medium saucepan; heat over medium heat. Add flour; cook and stir 1 minute. Add broth; simmer until thickened, stirring constantly. Spoon off fat from remaining pan drippings and discard. Add drippings to gravy. Stir in half-and-half, salt and pepper.

5. Remove and discard turkey skin. Carve turkey and transfer to serving platter. Serve with gravy. *Makes 14 servings*

Nutrients per Serving: Calories: 273, Calories from Fat: 28%, Total Fat: 8g, Saturated Fat: 2g, Cholesterol: 181mg, Sodium: 360mg, Carbohydrate: 2g, Fiber: <1g, Protein: 44g

·Fish·
& Shellfish

Grilled Caramelized Salmon and Asparagus

- **1 salmon fillet with skin (about 1 pound and 1 inch thick)**
- **2 tablespoons packed brown sugar**
- **1 tablespoon grated orange peel**
- **1 teaspoon minced garlic**
- **$\frac{1}{2}$ teaspoon salt**
- **$\frac{1}{8}$ to $\frac{1}{4}$ teaspoon ground red pepper**
- **Nonstick cooking spray**
- **16 asparagus spears, trimmed**
- **$\frac{1}{4}$ teaspoon black pepper**
- **1 cup finely chopped fresh pineapple**

1. Place salmon, skin side down, in shallow dish. Combine brown sugar, orange peel, garlic, salt and red pepper in small bowl. Rub onto salmon. Cover and refrigerate 2 to 8 hours.

2. Spray grill grid with cooking spray. Prepare grill for direct cooking.

3. Spray asparagus with cooking spray. Sprinkle with black pepper.

4. Grill salmon, skin side down, covered, over medium heat 6 minutes. Place asparagus on grid. Grill, covered, turning asparagus occasionally, 4 minutes or until salmon begins to flake when tested with fork and asparagus begins to brown.

5. Cut salmon into four equal pieces. Top salmon with pineapple and serve with asparagus.   *Makes 4 servings*

Nutrients per Serving: Calories: 277, Calories from Fat: 39%, Total Fat: 12g, Saturated Fat: 3g, Cholesterol: 66mg, Sodium: 363mg, Carbohydrate: 17g, Fiber: 3g, Protein: 25g

Lemon Shrimp with Black Beans and Rice

1 cup uncooked instant brown rice
$1/8$ teaspoon ground turmeric
1 pound raw shrimp, peeled and deveined, with tails on
$1^{1}/_{2}$ teaspoons chili powder
$1/2$ (15-ounce) can reduced-sodium black beans, rinsed and drained
1 medium poblano pepper *or* **$1/2$ green bell pepper, minced**
$1^{1}/_{2}$ to 2 teaspoons grated lemon peel
3 tablespoons lemon juice
$1^{1}/_{2}$ tablespoons extra virgin olive oil
$1/8$ teaspoon salt
Lemon wedges (optional)

1. Cook rice with turmeric according to package directions, omitting salt and fat.

2. Spray large nonstick skillet with nonstick cooking spray; heat over medium heat. Add shrimp and chili powder; cook and stir 4 minutes or until shrimp are pink and opaque. Add beans, pepper, lemon peel, lemon juice, oil and salt; cook and stir 1 minute or until heated through.

3. Spoon shrimp mixture over rice. Garnish with lemon wedges.

Makes 4 servings

Nutrients per Serving: Calories: 306, Calories from Fat: 23%, Total Fat: 8g, Saturated Fat: 1g, Cholesterol: 172mg, Sodium: 371mg, Carbohydrate: 33g, Fiber: 4g, Protein: 28g

Lemon Shrimp with Black Beans and Rice

Clam and Spinach Spaghetti

4 ounces uncooked multigrain spaghetti
2 teaspoons olive oil
1 cup diced onion
$1/4$ cup sliced green onions
1 clove garlic, minced
1 can ($6^1/2$ ounces) clams, undrained
2 cups baby spinach leaves
2 tablespoons shredded Parmesan cheese
2 tablespoons chopped fresh parsley *or* 2 teaspoons dried parsley
    Black pepper

1. Prepare pasta according to package directions, omitting salt and fat. Drain and keep warm.

2. Meanwhile, heat oil in large skillet over medium heat. Add onion; cook and stir about 2 minutes or until translucent. Add green onions and garlic; cook and stir 1 minute.

3. Add clams with juice; reduce heat to medium-low. Heat 1 to 2 minutes. Stir in spinach. Cover and cook about 2 minutes or until spinach wilts.

4. Serve clam mixture over pasta. Sprinkle with Parmesan, parsley and pepper.

Makes 3 servings

Nutrients per Serving: Calories: 293, Calories from Fat: 17%, Total Fat: 6g, Saturated Fat: 1g, Cholesterol: 44mg, Sodium: 151mg, Carbohydrate: 38g, Fiber: 3g, Protein: 24g

Clam and Spinach Spaghetti

• Fish & Shellfish •

Jerk Fish Tacos

$^1/_2$ **cup chopped peeled fresh mango (about** $^1/_2$ **medium mango)**
$^1/_2$ **cup canned black beans, rinsed and drained**
  1 tablespoon chopped fresh parsley
  1 tablespoon sliced green onion
  1 tablespoon finely chopped seeded jalapeño pepper* (optional)
  1 tablespoon frozen orange juice concentrate
  1 teaspoon olive oil
$2^1/_2$ **teaspoons Jamaican jerk seasoning**
  1 pound fresh or thawed frozen halibut steaks, cut 1 inch thick
  4 (7-inch) flour tortillas, warmed
  4 leaves romaine lettuce

*Jalapeño peppers can sting and irritate the skin, so wear rubber gloves when handling peppers and do not touch your eyes.

1. Preheat broiler. Combine mango, beans, parsley, green onion, jalapeño pepper, if desired, and orange juice concentrate in small bowl. Set aside.

2. Rub oil and jerk seasoning on both sides of fish. Place on rack of broiler pan. Broil 8 to 12 minutes or until fish begins to flake when tested with fork, turning once. Remove and discard skin and bones. Break fish into large bite-size pieces.

3. Fill tortillas with fish, mango mixture and lettuce.   *Makes 4 servings*

Nutrients per Serving: Calories: 279, Calories from Fat: 21%, Total Fat: 6g, Saturated Fat: 1g, Cholesterol: 36mg, Sodium: 678mg, Carbohydrate: 28g, Fiber: 3g, Protein: 28g

Jerk Fish Taco

Salmon-Potato Cakes with Mustard Tartar Sauce

3 small unpeeled red potatoes (8 ounces), halved
1 cup water
1 cup flaked cooked salmon
2 green onions, chopped
1 egg white
2 tablespoons chopped fresh parsley, divided
¹/₂ teaspoon Cajun or Creole seasoning mix
1 teaspoon olive or canola oil
1 tablespoon reduced-fat mayonnaise
1 tablespoon plain fat-free yogurt or fat-free sour cream
2 teaspoons coarse-grain mustard
1 tablespoon chopped dill pickle
1 teaspoon lemon juice

1. Place potatoes and water in medium saucepan. Bring to a boil. Reduce heat and simmer about 15 minutes or until potatoes are tender. Drain. Mash potatoes with fork, leaving chunky texture.

2. Combine mashed potatoes, salmon, green onions, egg white, 1 tablespoon parsley and seasoning mix in medium bowl.

3. Heat oil in medium nonstick skillet over medium heat. Gently shape salmon mixture into two patties. Place in skillet; flatten slightly. Cook 7 minutes or until browned and heated through, turning halfway through cooking time.

4. Meanwhile, combine mayonnaise, yogurt, mustard, remaining 1 tablespoon parsley, pickle and lemon juice in small bowl. Serve sauce with cakes.

Makes 2 servings

Nutrients per Serving: Calories: 276, Calories from Fat: 37%, Total Fat: 11g, Saturated Fat: 2g, Cholesterol: 52mg, Sodium: 300mg, Carbohydrate: 24g, Fiber: 2g, Protein: 19g

• Fish & Shellfish •

Fresh Garlic Shrimp Linguine

  6 ounces uncooked multigrain linguine or spaghetti, broken in half
  ½ pound raw shrimp, peeled and deveined
  ¼ cup grated Parmesan cheese
  3 tablespoons diet margarine
  1 clove garlic, minced
  ½ teaspoon seafood seasoning
  ¼ cup finely chopped fresh parsley (optional)
  ⅛ teaspoon salt (optional)

1. Cook linguine according to package directions, omitting salt and fat, about 7 minutes or until al dente. Add shrimp; cook 3 to 4 minutes or until shrimp are pink and opaque. Drain; transfer to medium bowl.

2. Add Parmesan, margarine, garlic and seafood seasoning; toss gently to coat. Add parsley and salt, if desired; toss to combine. *Makes 4 servings*

Nutrients per Serving (1 cup): Calories: 270, Calories from Fat: 25%, Total Fat: 7g, Saturated Fat: 2g, Cholesterol: 91mg, Sodium: 242mg, Carbohydrate: 30g, Fiber: 3g, Protein: 21g

Roasted Almond Tilapia

  2 tilapia or Boston scrod fillets (6 ounces each)
  ¼ teaspoon salt
  1 tablespoon prepared mustard
  ¼ cup whole wheat bread crumbs
  2 tablespoons chopped almonds
    Paprika (optional)
    Lemon wedges (optional)

1. Preheat oven to 450°F. Place fish on small baking sheet; season with salt. Spread mustard over fish. Combine bread crumbs and almonds in small bowl; sprinkle over fish. Press lightly to adhere. Sprinkle with paprika, if desired.

2. Bake 8 to 10 minutes or until fish begins to flake when tested with fork. Serve with lemon wedges, if desired. *Makes 2 servings*

Nutrients per Serving: Calories: 268, Calories from Fat: 32%, Total Fat: 10g, Saturated Fat: <1g, Cholesterol: 0mg, Sodium: 587mg, Carbohydrate: 14g, Fiber: 2g, Protein: 32g

Fresh Garlic Shrimp Linguine

• Fish & Shellfish •

Tuna Noodle Casserole

8 ounces uncooked wide cholesterol-free whole wheat egg noodles
$\frac{1}{2}$ cup finely chopped onion
1 can (10 ounces) reduced-fat condensed cream of mushroom soup, undiluted
$\frac{1}{2}$ cup reduced-fat sour cream
$\frac{1}{2}$ cup low-fat (1%) milk
$\frac{1}{8}$ teaspoon ground red pepper
12 ounces white tuna packed in water, drained and broken into chunks
$1\frac{1}{2}$ cups frozen baby peas
1 slice whole wheat or multigrain bread
$\frac{1}{2}$ teaspoon paprika

1. Preheat oven to 350°F. Spray 2½-quart casserole with nonstick cooking spray. Cook noodles according to package directions, omitting salt and fat. Drain; return to saucepan.

2. Meanwhile, spray large skillet with cooking spray. Add onion; cook and stir over medium heat 4 to 5 minutes or until tender. Stir in soup, sour cream, milk and red pepper until well blended. Add soup mixture, tuna and peas to noodles. Toss well; transfer mixture to prepared casserole.

3. Tear bread into pieces; place in food processor. Process until finely ground. Sprinkle over casserole; top with paprika.

4. Bake 30 to 35 minutes or until heated through.   *Makes 6 servings*

Nutrients per Serving: Calories: 315, Calories from Fat: 16%, Total Fat: 5g, Saturated Fat: 2g, Cholesterol: 31mg, Sodium: 502mg, Carbohydrate: 41g, Fiber: 4g, Protein: 23g

Tuna Noodle Casserole

• Fish & Shellfish •

Halibut with Peppers

1¼ cups reduced-sodium chicken broth, divided
½ cup diced yellow onion
2 teaspoons grated lemon peel
¼ teaspoon salt
⅛ teaspoon black pepper
1 pound halibut, cut into 4 (½-inch-thick) fillets
1 medium red bell pepper, cut into strips
1 medium yellow bell pepper, cut into strips
1 tablespoon lemon juice
2 teaspoons cornstarch
¼ cup sliced green onions
2 cups cooked couscous

1. Combine 1 cup broth, onion, lemon peel, salt and black pepper in large nonstick skillet. Bring to a boil over medium-high heat. Add fish; top with bell pepper strips. Reduce heat to medium-low. Cover and simmer 7 to 8 minutes or until fish begins to flake when tested with fork.

2. Use slotted spoon to transfer fish and bell peppers to plate, leaving liquid in skillet. Cover fish and bell peppers to keep warm. Measure liquid and add additional broth, if necessary, to equal ¾ cup. Return to skillet.

3. Combine remaining broth, lemon juice and cornstarch in small bowl until blended. Stir into liquid in skillet. Cook and stir over medium-high heat until boiling and slightly thickened. Stir in green onions.

4. Arrange fish and bell peppers over couscous. Top with lemon sauce.

Makes 4 servings

Nutrients per Serving: Calories: 259, Calories from Fat: 10%, Total Fat: 3g, Saturated Fat: <1g, Cholesterol: 38mg, Sodium: 258mg, Carbohydrate: 27g, Fiber: 3g, Protein: 29g

•Fish & Shellfish•

Rosemary-Garlic Scallops with Polenta

 2 teaspoons olive oil
 1 medium red bell pepper, cut into strips
 ⅓ cup chopped red onion
 3 cloves garlic, minced
 ½ pound fresh bay scallops
 2 teaspoons chopped fresh rosemary *or* ¾ teaspoon dried rosemary
 ¼ teaspoon black pepper
 1¼ cups fat-free reduced-sodium chicken broth
 ½ cup cornmeal
 ¼ teaspoon salt

1. Heat oil in large nonstick skillet over medium heat. Add bell pepper, onion and garlic; cook and stir 5 minutes. Add scallops, rosemary and black pepper; cook 3 to 5 minutes or until scallops are opaque, stirring occasionally.

2. Meanwhile, combine broth, cornmeal and salt in small saucepan. Bring to a boil over high heat. Reduce heat to low; simmer 5 minutes or until polenta is very thick, stirring frequently. Top polenta with scallop mixture. *Makes 2 servings*

Nutrients per Serving: Calories: 304, Calories from Fat: 23%, Total Fat: 8g, Saturated Fat: 1g, Cholesterol: 53mg, Sodium: 731mg, Carbohydrate: 33g, Fiber: 4g, Protein: 26g

There are two common varieties of scallops: bay and sea. Bay scallops are smaller and usually average about 100 per pound. Sea scallops are much larger, averaging about 30 per pound. Sea scallops cut into halves or thirds can easily substitute for bay scallops if the latter are not available.

·Meatless· Mains

Chunky Italian Stew with White Beans

1 teaspoon olive oil
2 green bell peppers, cut into $^3/_4$-inch pieces
1 yellow squash,* cut into $^3/_4$-inch pieces
1 zucchini,* cut into $^3/_4$-inch pieces
1 onion, cut into $^3/_4$-inch pieces
4 ounces mushrooms, quartered (about 1 cup)
1 can (about 15 ounces) reduced-sodium navy beans, rinsed and drained
1 can (about 14 ounces) reduced-sodium diced tomatoes
1 teaspoon dried oregano
$^1/_2$ teaspoon sugar
$^1/_2$ teaspoon Italian seasoning
$^1/_8$ teaspoon red pepper flakes (optional)
$^3/_4$ cup (3 ounces) shredded part-skim mozzarella cheese
1 tablespoon grated Parmesan cheese

Or, use 2 zucchini or 2 yellow squash instead of 1 each, if desired.

1. Heat oil in Dutch oven or large saucepan over medium-high heat. Add bell peppers, squash, zucchini, onion and mushrooms; cook and stir 8 minutes or until onion is translucent. Stir in beans, tomatoes, oregano, sugar, Italian seasoning and red pepper flakes, if desired. Reduce heat; cover and simmer 15 minutes or until vegetables are tender, stirring once.

2. Top with cheeses just before serving. *Makes 4 servings*

Nutrients per Serving: Calories: 265, Calories from Fat: 19%, Total Fat: 6g, Saturated Fat: 3g, Cholesterol: 15mg, Sodium: 208mg, Carbohydrate: 38g, Fiber: 9g, Protein: 17g

Grilled Portobello and Spring Green Sandwiches

2 tablespoons extra virgin olive oil
1½ tablespoons balsamic vinegar
1 tablespoon coarse-grain Dijon mustard
1 tablespoon water
1 teaspoon dried oregano
1 clove garlic, minced
½ teaspoon black pepper
¼ teaspoon salt
4 large portobello mushroom caps, wiped with damp towel, gills and stems removed
  Nonstick cooking spray
8 slices multigrain Italian bread (8 ounces)
¼ cup (1 ounce) crumbled reduced-fat blue cheese
2 to 3 ounces spring greens

1. Combine oil, vinegar, mustard, water, oregano, garlic, pepper and salt in medium bowl. Place mushrooms on sheet of foil or large plate. Brush 2 tablespoons dressing over mushrooms; set aside remaining dressing. Let mushrooms stand 30 minutes.

2. Spray grill pan with cooking spray; heat over medium-high heat. Spray both sides of bread slices with cooking spray. Grill bread 1 minute per side, pressing down with spatula to flatten slightly. Set aside.

3. Grill mushrooms 3 to 4 minutes per side or until tender. Place each mushroom on one bread slice. Sprinkle with blue cheese.

4. Combine spring greens and reserved dressing. Arrange spring greens on top of mushrooms; top with remaining bread slices. *Makes 4 servings*

Nutrients per Serving: Calories: 275, Calories from Fat: 33%, Total Fat: 10g, Saturated Fat: 2g, Cholesterol: 4mg, Sodium: 590mg, Carbohydrate: 36g, Fiber: 3g, Protein: 9g

Grilled Portobello and Spring Green Sandwiches

•Meatless **Mains**•

Take-and-Shake Salad

1 can (about 15 ounces) low-sodium chickpeas, rinsed and drained
1 pint cherry tomatoes (sweet grape variety), halved
1 can (14 ounces) quartered artichoke hearts, drained
4 ounces crumbled low-fat feta cheese
4 ounces sliced mushrooms
1 can ($2^{1}/_{4}$ ounces) sliced black olives, drained
$^{1}/_{2}$ medium green bell pepper, chopped
$^{2}/_{3}$ cup cider vinegar
$1^{1}/_{2}$ tablespoons extra virgin olive oil
2 packets sugar substitute
1 teaspoon dried oregano
$^{1}/_{4}$ teaspoon black pepper
5 cups chopped romaine lettuce

1. Combine chickpeas, tomatoes, artichoke hearts, feta, mushrooms, olives and bell pepper in large bowl; toss gently to blend. Divide chickpea mixture among five gallon-sized resealable food storage bags.

2. Combine vinegar, oil, sugar substitute, oregano and black pepper in small bowl; whisk until well blended. Spoon 3 tablespoons dressing into each of five small resealable food storage bags. Seal and place one in each salad bag. Seal and refrigerate until needed.

3. Add 1 cup lettuce to each salad just before serving.

4. Pour dressing over salad. Seal bag and toss to coat. *Makes 5 servings*

Nutrients per Serving: Calories: 305, Calories from Fat: 31%, Total Fat: 11g, Saturated Fat: 3g, Cholesterol: 8mg, Sodium: 648mg, Carbohydrate: 39g, Fiber: 9g, Protein: 17g

Take-and-Shake Salad

• Meatless **Mains** •

Mediterranean Veggies with Navy Bean Penne

4 ounces uncooked multigrain penne pasta
1 can (about 15 ounces) no-salt-added navy beans, rinsed and drained
1 medium green bell pepper, chopped
1 small zucchini (about 5 ounces), sliced
2 cloves garlic, minced
1 can (about 14 ounces) stewed tomatoes
2 teaspoons dried basil
2 teaspoons extra virgin olive oil
1/2 cup (2 ounces) shredded mozzarella cheese
1 tablespoon plus 1 teaspoon grated Parmesan cheese

1. Cook pasta according to package directions, omitting salt and fat; add beans during last minute of cooking. Drain and keep warm.

2. Meanwhile, heat large nonstick skillet over medium-high heat. Spray skillet with nonstick cooking spray. Add bell pepper and zucchini; cook 5 minutes or until beginning to brown on edges, stirring frequently. Add garlic; cook 15 seconds, stirring constantly. Add tomatoes and basil; bring to a boil over high heat. Reduce heat to low; cover and simmer 10 minutes. Stir in oil.

3. Spoon tomato mixture over pasta mixture; sprinkle with cheeses.

Makes 5 servings

Nutrients per Serving: Calories: 296, Calories from Fat: 18%, Total Fat: 6g, Saturated Fat: 2g, Cholesterol: 7mg, Sodium: 376mg, Carbohydrate: 48g, Fiber: 13g, Protein: 16g

• Meatless **Mains** •

One-for-All Veggie Sub

$^1/_2$ **(15-ounce) can navy beans, rinsed and drained**
$^1/_3$ **cup chipotle salsa**
  1 to 2 tablespoons red wine vinegar
$^1/_2$ **to 1 tablespoon dried oregano**
  1 clove garlic
  1 round multigrain Italian bread (1 pound)
  1 medium tomato, thinly sliced
  1 cup packed spring greens
$^1/_2$ **small red onion, thinly sliced**
  1 Anaheim pepper or small green bell pepper, thinly sliced
$^3/_4$ **cup (3 ounces) crumbled reduced-fat feta cheese**

1. Combine beans, salsa, vinegar, oregano and garlic in food processor; process until smooth.

2. Cut bread in half horizontally. Hollow out top and bottom halves of bread, leaving $^1/_2$-inch-thick shell; reserve torn bread for another use.

3. Spread bean mixture evenly on cut sides of bread. Arrange tomato slices over bottom half of bread. Top with greens, onion, pepper and feta. Cover with top half of bread. Cut filled loaf into wedges. *Makes 6 servings*

Nutrients per Serving: Calories: 257, Calories from Fat: 11%, Total Fat: 3g, Saturated Fat: 2g, Cholesterol: 4mg, Sodium: 614mg, Carbohydrate: 45g, Fiber: 6g, Protein: 13g

• Meatless **Mains** •

Barley and Swiss Chard Skillet Casserole

1 cup water
1 cup chopped red bell pepper
1 cup chopped green bell pepper
¾ cup uncooked quick-cooking barley
⅛ teaspoon garlic powder
⅛ teaspoon red pepper flakes
2 cups packed coarsely chopped Swiss chard*
1 cup canned reduced-sodium navy beans, rinsed and drained
1 cup quartered cherry tomatoes
¼ cup chopped fresh basil leaves
1 tablespoon olive oil
2 tablespoons Italian-seasoned dry bread crumbs

*Fresh spinach or beet greens can be substituted for Swiss chard.

1. Preheat broiler.

2. Bring water to a boil in large ovenproof skillet; add bell peppers, barley, garlic powder and red pepper flakes. Reduce heat; cover and simmer 10 minutes or until liquid is absorbed. Remove from heat.

3. Stir in chard, beans, tomatoes, basil and oil. Sprinkle with bread crumbs. Broil 2 minutes or until golden.   *Makes 4 servings*

Nutrients per Serving (1¼ cups): Calories: 288, Calories from Fat: 18%, Total Fat: 6g, Saturated Fat: <1g, Cholesterol: 0mg, Sodium: 488mg, Carbohydrate: 45g, Fiber: 12g, Protein: 10g

•Meatless **Mains**•

Peanut-Sauced Pasta

 1/3 cup vegetable broth
 3 tablespoons creamy peanut butter
 2 tablespoons seasoned rice vinegar
 2 tablespoons reduced-sodium soy sauce
 1/2 teaspoon red pepper flakes
 9 ounces uncooked multigrain linguine
 1 1/2 pounds fresh asparagus, cut into 1-inch pieces (4 cups)
 1/3 cup unsalted dry-roasted peanuts, chopped

1. Heat broth, peanut butter, vinegar, soy sauce and red pepper flakes in small saucepan over low heat, stirring frequently. Keep warm.

2. Cook pasta according to package directions, omitting salt and fat. Add asparagus during last 5 minutes of cooking. Drain. Toss with peanut sauce. Sprinkle with peanuts. *Makes 6 servings*

Nutrients per Serving (1 cup): Calories: 300, Calories from Fat: 33%, Total Fat: 11g, Saturated Fat: 2g, Cholesterol: 0mg, Sodium: 449mg, Carbohydrate: 38g, Fiber: 5g, Protein: 14g

Grilled Mozzarella & Roasted Red Pepper Sandwich

 1 tablespoon reduced-fat Italian salad dressing
 2 slices Italian-style sandwich bread (2 ounces)
 Fresh basil leaves (optional)
 1/3 cup roasted red peppers, rinsed, drained and patted dry
 1 to 2 slices (1 ounce each) part-skim mozzarella cheese
 Olive oil cooking spray

1. Brush dressing on one side of one bread slice; top with basil, if desired, roasted peppers, cheese and remaining bread slice. Lightly spray both sides of sandwich with cooking spray.

2. Cook sandwich in large nonstick skillet over medium heat 4 to 5 minutes per side or until cheese melts and sandwich is golden brown. *Makes 1 serving*

Nutrients per Serving: Calories: 303, Calories from Fat: 29%, Total Fat: 9g, Saturated Fat: 5g, Cholesterol: 25mg, Sodium: 727mg, Carbohydrate: 35g, Fiber: 2g, Protein: 16g

Peanut-Sauced Pasta

• Meatless **Mains** •

Couscous-Stuffed Squash

2 small acorn squash, halved lengthwise and seeded
1 medium poblano pepper, sliced
1 small onion, sliced
1¼ cups vegetable broth
½ cup shiitake mushrooms, chopped
¾ cup uncooked couscous
1 medium plum tomato, diced
2 tablespoons pine nuts

1. Preheat oven to 400°F. Spray baking sheet with nonstick cooking spray; place squash, cut sides down, on baking sheet. Spread pepper and onion on baking sheet. Cover with foil; bake 35 to 40 minutes or until squash is tender.

2. Bring broth and mushrooms to a boil in medium saucepan over medium-high heat. Stir in couscous, tomato and pine nuts; cover and remove from heat. Let stand 5 minutes. Meanwhile, dice roasted pepper and onion; add to couscous mixture, fluffing couscous lightly with fork.

3. Turn squash cut sides up. Fill with couscous mixture.   *Makes 4 servings*

Nutrients per Serving: Calories: 290, Calories from Fat: 12%, Total Fat: 4g, Saturated Fat: <1g, Cholesterol: 0mg, Sodium: 187mg, Carbohydrate: 57g, Fiber: 6g, Protein: 9g

Tip Acorn squash have thick, hard skins that can be difficult to cut. To make cutting squash easier, soften them in the microwave. Pierce the skin with a fork; microwave on HIGH 1 to 2 minutes. Allow to cool for a few minutes, then slice lengthwise and remove the seeds.

• Meatless **Mains** •

Chickpea Vegetable Curry

2 teaspoons canola oil
4 cups chopped fresh vegetables, such as bell peppers, broccoli, celery,
    carrots, zucchini and red onion
3 cloves garlic, minced
2 cups low-sodium vegetable broth, divided
1$^1/_2$ teaspoons curry powder
$^1/_4$ teaspoon ground red pepper
1 can (about 15 ounces) no-salt-added chickpeas, undrained
$^1/_3$ cup golden raisins
$^1/_4$ to $^1/_2$ teaspoon salt (optional)
$^3/_4$ cup uncooked whole wheat couscous
$^1/_4$ cup chopped fresh cilantro
$^1/_4$ cup sliced almonds, toasted (optional)

1. Heat oil in large saucepan over medium heat. Add vegetables; cook 5 minutes, stirring occasionally. Add garlic; cook 1 minute. Stir in 1 cup broth, curry powder and red pepper. Bring to a boil. Reduce heat; cover and simmer 6 minutes. Stir in chickpeas, raisins and salt, if desired; cover and simmer 2 to 3 minutes or until vegetables are tender.

2. Meanwhile, bring remaining 1 cup broth to a boil in small saucepan over medium-high heat. Stir in couscous. Cover and remove from heat. Let stand 5 minutes. Stir in cilantro and almonds, if desired. Serve curry over couscous.   *Makes 4 servings*

Tip: To toast almonds, spread in small nonstick skillet. Cook over medium heat 3 to 5 minutes or until lightly browned, stirring constantly. Transfer to plate to cool.

Nutrients per Serving: Calories: 291, Calories from Fat: 15%, Total Fat: 5g, Saturated Fat: <1g, Cholesterol: 0mg, Sodium: 113mg, Carbohydrate: 51g, Fiber: 12g, Protein: 14g

Chickpea Vegetable Curry

• Meatless **Mains** •

Chickpea and Orange Squash Stew

 1 teaspoon canola oil
 ³/₄ cup chopped onion
 ¹/₂ to 1 jalapeño pepper,* seeded and minced
 ¹/₂ inch fresh ginger, peeled and minced
 1 clove garlic, minced
 2 teaspoons ground cumin
 ¹/₂ teaspoon ground coriander
 1 cup cubed peeled orange squash, sweet potato or pumpkin
 1 cup canned low-sodium chickpeas, rinsed and drained
 ¹/₂ cup water
 ¹/₂ tablespoon reduced-sodium soy sauce
 1 cup reduced-fat coconut milk
 Juice of 1 lime
 ¹/₄ cup chopped fresh cilantro
 Baby spinach leaves (optional)

*Jalapeño peppers can sting and irritate the skin, so wear rubber gloves when handling peppers and do not touch your eyes.

1. Heat oil in medium saucepan over medium-low heat. Add onion, jalapeño pepper, ginger and garlic; cook and stir 2 to 3 minutes or until onion is translucent. Add cumin and coriander; cook and stir 1 minute.

2. Add squash, chickpeas, water and soy sauce to saucepan. Bring to a boil. Reduce heat and simmer 15 minutes or until squash is tender. Add coconut milk; cook and stir 2 to 3 minutes or until heated through. Stir in lime juice and cilantro. Garnish with spinach. *Makes 2 servings*

Nutrients per Serving: Calories: 300, Calories from Fat: 33%, Total Fat: 11g, Saturated Fat: 4g, Cholesterol: 0mg, Sodium: 204mg, Carbohydrate: 42g, Fiber: 10g, Protein: 10g

•Index•

• Index •

·Index·

•Index•

•Index•

•Index•

Index

• Index •

· Index ·

•Index•

Metric Conversion Chart

VOLUME MEASUREMENTS (dry)

1/8 teaspoon = 0.5 mL
1/4 teaspoon = 1 mL
1/2 teaspoon = 2 mL
3/4 teaspoon = 4 mL
1 teaspoon = 5 mL
1 tablespoon = 15 mL
2 tablespoons = 30 mL
1/4 cup = 60 mL
1/3 cup = 75 mL
1/2 cup = 125 mL
2/3 cup = 150 mL
3/4 cup = 175 mL
1 cup = 250 mL
2 cups = 1 pint = 500 mL
3 cups = 750 mL
4 cups = 1 quart = 1 L

VOLUME MEASUREMENTS (fluid)

1 fluid ounce (2 tablespoons) = 30 mL
4 fluid ounces (1/2 cup) = 125 mL
8 fluid ounces (1 cup) = 250 mL
12 fluid ounces (1 1/2 cups) = 375 mL
16 fluid ounces (2 cups) = 500 mL

WEIGHTS (mass)

1/2 ounce = 15 g
1 ounce = 30 g
3 ounces = 90 g
4 ounces = 120 g
8 ounces = 225 g
10 ounces = 285 g
12 ounces = 360 g
16 ounces = 1 pound = 450 g

DIMENSIONS

1/16 inch = 2 mm
1/8 inch = 3 mm
1/4 inch = 6 mm
1/2 inch = 1.5 cm
3/4 inch = 2 cm
1 inch = 2.5 cm

OVEN TEMPERATURES

250°F = 120°C
275°F = 140°C
300°F = 150°C
325°F = 160°C
350°F = 180°C
375°F = 190°C
400°F = 200°C
425°F = 220°C
450°F = 230°C

BAKING PAN SIZES

Utensil	Size in Inches/Quarts	Metric Volume	Size in Centimeters
Baking or Cake Pan (square or rectangular)	8×8×2	2 L	20×20×5
	9×9×2	2.5 L	23×23×5
	12×8×2	3 L	30×20×5
	13×9×2	3.5 L	33×23×5
Loaf Pan	8×4×3	1.5 L	20×10×7
	9×5×3	2 L	23×13×7
Round Layer Cake Pan	8×1½	1.2 L	20×4
	9×1½	1.5 L	23×4
Pie Plate	8×1¼	750 mL	20×3
	9×1¼	1 L	23×3
Baking Dish or Casserole	1 quart	1 L	—
	1½ quart	1.5 L	—
	2 quart	2 L	—